A HOAX
BY RICK VIEDE

CURRENCY PRESS
SYDNEY

GRIFFIN THE COMPANY

CURRENCY PLAYS

First published in 2012
by Currency Press Pty Ltd,
PO Box 2287, Strawberry Hills, NSW, 2012, Australia
enquiries@currency.com.au
www.currency.com.au

in association with Griffin Theatre Company

NATIONAL LIBRARY OF AUSTRALIA CIP DATA

Author:	Viede, Rick.
Title:	A hoax / Rick Viede.
ISBN:	9780868199481 (pbk.)
Series:	Current theatre series.
Subject:	Australian drama—21st century.
Dewey Number:	A822.4

Typeset by Dean Nottle for Currency Press.
Printed by Hyde Park Press, Richmond SA.
Cover photograph by Katie Kaars. Cover design by Interbrand.
Front cover shows Shari Sebbens.

Contents

Theatre Program at the end of the playtext

A Hoax was first produced by La Boite Theatre Company, in association with Griffin Theatre Company, at Roundhouse Theatre, Brisbane, on 5 May 2012, with the following cast:

TYRELLE PARKS	Charles Allen
ANTHONY DOOLEY	Glenn Hazeldine
RONNIE LOWE	Sally McKenzie
MIRI SMITH / CURRAH	Shari Sebbens

Director, Lee Lewis
Dramaturg, Tahli Corin
Designer, Renée Mulder
Design Assistant, Melita Lee Yuen
Music, Sound & A/V Designer, Steve Toulmin
Fight Choreographer, Nigel Poulton

CHARACTERS

MIRI SMITH / CURRAH, early 20s, Indigenous Australian *

ANTHONY DOOLEY, early/mid 30s, Caucasian

RONNIE LOWE, early 60s, Caucasian

TYRELLE PARKS, 30s, African American

* For ease of recognition, when Miri is playing the part of Currah the dialogue is attributed to Currah.

SETTING

The play can be set in any major city around the world, but the part of Currah was written for an Aboriginal Australian.

PLAYWRIGHT'S NOTE

There are numerous kinds of literary hoaxes and numerous reasons why they are committed. This play concerns the growing market need for 'misery memoirs' and the writers who have created stories to fulfill that need, for varying personal purposes. The hoaxes notably include the cases of J.T. Leroy, Anthony Godby Johnson, Wanda Koolmatrie and Nasdijj, and two bestselling memoirists accused of heavily manipulating the truth for their own (commercial) gain, James Frey and Dave Pelzer.

It is worth noting how many of those writers play with gender, race and sexuality in the creation of their alter egos.

This play is, however, a fiction.

This play went to press before the end of rehearsals and may differ from the play as performed.

ACT ONE

Various extracts from CURRAH's *freshly submitted short stories.*
Words fly through the air, maybe with corresponding visual imagery.
We never see CURRAH's *face. But we do hear her voice.*
And occasionally the voice of an unknown male. He is never seen.

CURRAH: Do you ever think / you're nothing?

MAN: Do you ever think you're nothing?

CURRAH: I do.

MAN & CURRAH: [*together*] All the time.

CURRAH: Don't put me back in that cellar!

MAN: Looked like I was wearing plaid stockings made from blood. All those cuts.

CURRAH: Mum got stolen by a bunch / of white blokes when she was kid.

MAN: Mum got stolen from me when a truck crushed her Datsun.

CURRAH: Mum liked being stole.

MAN: Don't put me back in that cellar.

CURRAH: All I got is / this piece of paper and this pen.

MAN: All I got is this piece of paper and this pen.

CURRAH: He did me good for that.

MAN: You're a / special one, Currah.

CURRAH: You're a special one.

MAN: You're gonna be sexy and you gonna show us all how it should be done.

CURRAH: Like Lena Horne or Dorothy Dandridge.
Often I think that / I am nothing.

MAN: I am nothing.

CURRAH: You see, my name is / Currah.

MAN: My name is Currah and I'm Nobody's / Girl.

CURRAH: I'm Nobody's Girl.

♦ ♦ ♦ ♦ ♦

A room in a Travelodge hotel.

A door to the hallway sits centre stage. A bed. A couch with several chairs. A loaded minibar. Another door leads to the bathroom. A basic hotel room, but essentially pleasant.

A knock on the door.

ANTHONY *looks up nervously.*

Beat.

Another knock on the door.

ANTHONY: Who is it?

MIRI: It's me.

ANTHONY: Who's me?

MIRI: Who do you think?

ANTHONY: Miri Smith?

MIRI: Well, I'm not the Queen Mother.

ANTHONY: You know she's dead?

     He opens the door.

  The Queen Mother is dead.

MIRI: I knew that.

  I did know that.

ANTHONY: So did I.

MIRI: What?

ANTHONY: I knew she was dead.

MIRI: That's why you said it.

ANTHONY: Yes.

  Yes.

     Beat.

MIRI: Do ya just want me to stand in the hallway?

ANTHONY: What?

MIRI: Give us a look—?

ANTHONY: Oh. Yes—come in.

  You haven't told anyone you're here?

MIRI: [*looking at the room*] Holy fuck—

  Look at this place.

ANTHONY: No-one knows, do they—

MIRI: This is where they put you?

ANTHONY: Now I hope you didn't tell anyone—

MIRI: You even have your own bathroom?

  She goes to investigate.

ANTHONY: What are you doing?

  You haven't seen a hotel room before?

MIRI: No.

ANTHONY: Did you need something to eat?

MIRI: I'm fine—I brought my own—

  She goes to her bag and gets a packet of chips.

ANTHONY: I can get you something to eat?

MIRI: Did you want some chips?

ANTHONY: What?

MIRI: They're the good kind. Balsamic vinegar and sea salt.

ANTHONY: I just had room service.

  But thank you for thinking of me.

MIRI: You can get that here?

ANTHONY: Room service? Yes. I got steak.

MIRI: They gave you steak?

ANTHONY: Yeah.

MIRI: Right.

  So—Anthony—

ANTHONY: Call me Ant. That's what my friends call me.

MIRI: Ant?

ANTHONY: Everyone outside of work calls me Ant.

MIRI: Nah. You're Anthony.

ANTHONY: Yeah, well, trust me—I'm totally an Ant, okay—it's what everyone calls me.

  I really want to thank you for doing this—

MIRI: So, Ant—

ANTHONY: I just want you to know that I really appreciate it—and I have the utmost respect for you.

MIRI: Should we sort this out now?

ANTHONY: What?

MIRI: The money—

ANTHONY: Course.

No really—I want you to know I very much respect you.

ANTHONY *pulls out his wallet—counts off four fifty-dollar notes.*

MIRI *takes off her jacket and sits on the bed.*

MIRI: So how much would this all cost?

ANTHONY: What—the room?

MIRI: Yeah.

ANTHONY: I dunno—

One hundred—one fifty maybe?

MIRI: For a night.

Or a week?

ANTHONY: A night.

MIRI: Wow. So that'd be like—eight, nine hundred bucks for a week? How long you been here?

ANTHONY: I'm just here tonight.

MIRI: Nice.

ANTHONY: Um—so here you go—

This is what we agreed.

MIRI: Ta.

So it's just this one time then?

ANTHONY: Yes—just this one time—

MIRI: It's cool if you want me to do it again—

ANTHONY: Thank you—

MIRI: 'Cause hey, I'm totally up for this whenever you need—like any time, you know?

ANTHONY: I'll make sure I keep that in mind…

Beat.

You got the stuff I sent you—

MIRI: Oh yeah, I did—I liked it—well, the bits I read—

ANTHONY: I thought it would help you to understand how I want this to all play out—

MIRI: Yeah, totally—I really liked it—

ANTHONY: Because I want you to feel really comfortable doing this—

MIRI: It's pretty fucked up hey—

ANTHONY: I guess from a certain light it can be viewed like that.

MIRI: It's so funny.

ANTHONY: It's not meant to be funny.

MIRI: Nah, not funny, interesting, that's what I meant.

ANTHONY: There's nothing funny about it.

MIRI: Nah, course not, like it's totally sad you know.

ANTHONY: Yes—it's a very sad story—and that's the way you need to do it okay—It'll work much better if you're really sad—

MIRI: I totally think that too—totally totally sad—

I dunno why it made me laugh—guess I'm kinda stupid when it comes to this sort of shit.

ANTHONY: I'm sure you're not stupid—just maybe it's not the most appropriate reaction…

MIRI: Yeah, I guess not—

ANTHONY: Something to work on—right?

MIRI: Totally.

ANTHONY: And don't worry, I won't let you embarrass yourself or say something stupid.

Just let me do most of the talking, okay?

Beat.

MIRI: Course. You're paying.

Anyways it's kinda fun—flying in aeroplanes, getting to meet fancypants men in hotel rooms.

ANTHONY: Women.

MIRI: What?

ANTHONY: It's a woman you'll be meeting.

MIRI: You want me to do all this with a woman…

ANTHONY: She'll be here in about an hour. Her name's Ronnie Lowe.

MIRI: Ronnie Lowe.

ANTHONY: She's a big shot.

MIRI: So how do you know her?

ANTHONY: Everyone knows Ronnie Lowe.

MIRI: And she's the big fry?

ANTHONY: She's the real deal, yes.

MIRI: Fuck.

ANTHONY: If Ronnie signs Currah up to her agency—then Currah might get a publishing deal—and that means I'd get published. So all I need is for you to pretend to be Currah—don't do anything—don't say anything—just be really sad.

MIRI: Hey, can I have a shower?

ANTHONY: What?

MIRI: You know—a shower.

ANTHONY: Oh. Freshen up?

MIRI: Totally.

ANTHONY: Okay—well, it's just through there.

> *Beat.*

What?

MIRI: Some space?

ANTHONY: What?

MIRI: I don't want to shower with you in the room.

ANTHONY: Oh—

MIRI: What do you think I am?

ANTHONY: Oh. Sorry.

MIRI: Can you go for a walk or something?

ANTHONY: Fine—fine—

Twenty minutes?

MIRI: Thank you.

God.

ANTHONY: I'll be back in twenty minutes—

> ANTHONY *walks out the door.*

> MIRI *immediately runs around the room—jumps on the bed—lands on the remote control. She turns the aircon on and off.*

And then turns on the TV.

She channel surfs the cable until she finds the music channel.

Daggy 80s hip hop: Salt-N-Pepa's 'Push It'.

She laughs and cranks it REALLY, REALLY LOUD.

Dancing and singing, she moves to the minibar—looks at all the little bottles—empties a mini vodka and then…

Puts all the little bottles into her bag.

She dances and strips off her clothes—doing that thing you do when you're somewhere new and nice and different, it's not yours and you're totally alone…

She does her best Tom Cruise—Risky Business impersonation.

Naked, except for her underwear, she sings very loudly (she knows all the words).

She walks into the bathroom and we hear the shower turn on.

She continues to sing, very loudly, very badly, in the shower.

Beat.

A key card in the front door. The door swings open to reveal RONNIE LOWE. *A woman in her early sixties who knows how the world works.*

She moves into the room.

MIRI *is still singing loudly in the shower.*

RONNIE *allows herself a smile when she hears the singing and moves to the minibar, finding it sadly absent of any alcohol.*

She has a little snoop around the room, before having an idea and looking inside Miri's bag.

She takes out two mini bottles of scotch from the bag and pours them into her glass, neat.

She sits down on the sofa and waits.

The shower turns off.

Beat.

MIRI *walks out, dripping wet, a towel tied around her, still singing.*

RONNIE: [*over the music*] Currah, I presume?

　　MIRI *lets out a scream.*

MIRI: Who the fuck—?

RONNIE: There's no need to be frightened.

MIRI: How the fuck did you—?

RONNIE: It's just me—

MIRI: Who the fuck are you?

RONNIE: It's just me, Currah—

MIRI: What the fuck are you doing?

RONNIE: Can we just— [turn down the music]

MIRI: What the fuck?

RONNIE: Currah—can I just?

MIRI: Fine, fine, fucking fine!

　　　MIRI *turns off the TV.*

RONNIE: You'll make yourself deaf with that racket.

MIRI: Who the fuck are you?

RONNIE: There's no need to keep dropping the 'fuck' bomb.

MIRI: What the fuck are you doing in my room?

RONNIE: You know what I'm doing in your room—

MIRI: Haven't you heard of knocking?

RONNIE: It's me, Currah.

MIRI: It's fucking me…?

RONNIE: You know who.

　My little girl.

　　　Yes, MIRI *knows exactly who she is…*

　　　It's crunch time.

　　　MIRI *imperceptibly changes.*

CURRAH: You're that—that—

RONNIE: That's right. I'm Ronnie.

　It's a pleasure to finally meet you.

　　　She holds out her hand.

　　　Beat.

CURRAH *moves to shake it.*

CURRAH: You scared the shit out of me.

RONNIE: You sounded like you were having fun—

I didn't want to disturb you—

CURRAH: You shouldn't be here.

You're early.

RONNIE: I knew you'd checked in.

I wanted to be sure to get you.

I didn't want you to get cold feet like the last two times…

I've never been stood up twice before…

CURRAH: How did you get in here?

RONNIE: A key.

CURRAH: How did you get the key?

RONNIE: I paid for the room, Currah, how do you think I got the key?

Beat.

Now why don't you put on some clothes and come join me?

It's good to finally meet you.

CURRAH *moves to the bed, picks up some clothes and heads back into the bathroom.*

Do you like the room?

CURRAH: Yeah—it's nice.

RONNIE: Just nice?

CURRAH: It's real nice.

RONNIE: I'm so glad you like it.

You obviously found the TV?

CURRAH: Yeah, they've even got Foxtel!

RONNIE: [*dryly*] How fancy.

You ever stayed in a place like this before?

CURRAH: What do you think?

RONNIE: Well, I guess I thought no—no, you probably haven't.

I thought it might be a little treat.

Something a bit different for a very talented writer…

CURRAH *emerges—hair still wet, in tracky pants and a t-shirt.*

CURRAH: Yeah—thanks for all this—it's real—um—good.

RONNIE: Real. Um. Good.

What a wordsmith.

CURRAH: I'm sorry.

RONNIE: I'm quite excited, I must say.

And really—it's very rare I get excited these days.

Age, darling—don't do it.

Let me look at you.

Stand. Nice. Let me look.

> CURRAH *stands still,* RONNIE *inspecting her.*
>
> *Beat.*

CURRAH: Are you…?

RONNIE: Turn.

> CURRAH *turns.*

And there you are.

My Currah.

I didn't know what to expect. I half thought maybe you didn't exist—you know, sometimes people can just be too good to be true. But here you are.

CURRAH: Yep. You're looking right at me.

RONNIE: Can I get you a drink?

CURRAH: I—I—

RONNIE: What'll it be? Vodka? Scotch?

You *are* over eighteen, right?

CURRAH: Vodka.

> RONNIE *moves to Miri's bag and pulls out two vodka bottles and moves to the bar.*

RONNIE: And there's no need to go sneaking the minibar, is there?

I mean, it's adorable.

But there's no need.

CURRAH: Look, I'm really sorry, okay.

> *Beat.*

RONNIE: No, I'm sorry. I'm being a bitch.

Darling—always take the minibar.

And the soap and the fragrance and the shower hat (if they still have them), take anything that's not screwed down.

But don't you change a goddamned thing, my adorable little girl!

CURRAH: Why are you being nice to me?

RONNIE: Don't you deserve people to be nice to you?

CURRAH: People that are nice just want something.

> RONNIE *laughs.*

RONNIE: God, Currah. So cynical— (of course it's understandable with what you've been through…)

I'm just being nice to you because you deserve it.

You're a talent. I love talent.

CURRAH: You don't want nothing?

RONNIE: Just you to be you.

And of course to talk—we do need to talk—

There are so many exciting things I want to do with you—if you decide to join me?

> *A knock at the door.*

CURRAH: [*relieved*] That'll be Anthony.

RONNIE: Anthony?

CURRAH: You know—the—um—social worker dude that found me—

RONNIE: Oh yes—Anthony.

I didn't think he'd be here.

CURRAH: I just didn't want to be alone—

RONNIE: I don't know why—I'm not here to take advantage of you—

CURRAH: I know but—

RONNIE: You trust me, don't you—?

CURRAH: Yeah, but—I don't know you—

RONNIE: You've got to learn to trust me—I'm here just for you—

CURRAH: Can I? You know—open the door?

RONNIE: Please. Never let me stop you from doing what you want.

> CURRAH *opens the door.*

> TYRELLE *stands in the doorway, an immaculately dressed man.*

TYRELLE: Currah?! Currah?!

CURRAH: What—who are—?

TYRELLE: Currah!? OMFG!?

RONNIE: Tyrelle?

TYRELLE: I'm sorry, Ronnie—you said you were off to meet her—and well—I just *had* to see this girl in the flesh.

I'm your hugest fan.

RONNIE: For Christ's sake, Tyrelle!

TYRELLE: [*shaking* CURRAH*'s hand*] Hi there—Tyrelle—huge. Fan.

Huge.

Totally!

RONNIE: Weren't you meeting LeRoy?

TYRELLE: He's such a faggot. And it gets too crowded on the waterfront, you know—

Can I take a photo? Oh, you! How are *you*?

CURRAH: What—?

TYRELLE: She's overwhelmed—bless—let me explain.

As a biracial homosexual from a working-class background, and someone, might I add, who has been ridiculed enough for some of my more *outré* mannerisms, Currah—I gotta say it—I do. Your stories touched me.

CURRAH: What?

TYRELLE: Really touched me.

RONNIE: Don't mind him, darling—he can't help being like that.

TYRELLE: Fuck off, Ronnie—

Currah, really—you are the rage, darling—we all just want to know about this poor little black girl—

That one where you steel-wool yourself to find the white—or the tartan cuts—the crisscross—on your thigh—in the weather it still raises up—shit—

Gurl—we relate—we all relate to you—I relate—

RONNIE: Darling—you should know this by now—everyone *loves* how you write. We relate. I relate. I probably shouldn't—I'm a rich white woman who seemingly has it all—except for my appalling history of loving complete and utter bastards and so that story—*I related.*

TYRELLE: Mm-hmm.

RONNIE: It's true.

TYRELLE: Oh, honey, it's fierce. We've all been laying down bets who will be first to meet you—I have a friend—Beard. Lisp. Asshole. He said he'd met you? Did he? Did he meet you? I'll kill him. Fucking kill him.

> *Beat.*

CURRAH: Can I sit down?

> TYRELLE *bursts into laughter.*

TYRELLE: Bless—I've frightened her!

RONNIE: You come in screaming like some black happy clappy; next you'll be asking her if she's found Jesus.

TYRELLE: Shut your face, Ronnie.

But have you, Currah, found Jesus?

> *Beat.*

Joke!

CURRAH: Who are you?

RONNIE: This is Tyrelle. Works for my agency.

CURRAH: He's an agent?

TYRELLE: Oh, honey—do I look like that much of a bitch?

Shut your hole, Ronnie.

RONNIE: Tyrelle's been working as my assistant.

TYRELLE: For years.

But now I also go to night school!

RONNIE: [*bitchily*] How's the certificate going?

TYRELLE: It's a diploma?!

[*To* CURRAH] I'm going to be a journalist.

RONNIE: But let's not talk about Tyrelle—

TYRELLE: So I was thinking—quick interview?

RONNIE: Give me a break, Tyrelle.

He believes that my life consists of being a major bitch, but it's just not true. I do other things too.

TYRELLE: Eat the young?

CURRAH: You people are fucking shitting me?

TYRELLE: What?

RONNIE: No, honey, no—

(Tyrelle, back off—you're scaring her—)

Love.

I'm an agent—that means I'm here to represent my writers. Hopefully you, Currah.

I love my job. I adore protecting my writers. I live for it.

TYRELLE: It's true—she does—

RONNIE: I couldn't do anything else—

CURRAH: That's all you do?

Protect people?

RONNIE: Yes—

CURRAH: You're like a standover man?

RONNIE: Bless—sweet—yes—actually—

[*To* TYRELLE] I guess it's kinda similar—

All my clients call me Mama.

TYRELLE: Midas Mama.

RONNIE: They do not call me that—

TYRELLE: Everyone for years called her Midas Mama—

RONNIE: Oh, stop it, Tyrelle!

TYRELLE: For years—

RONNIE: I was known as Midas Mama.

CURRAH: Why?

　　　　Beat.

TYRELLE: Everything she touched turned to gold.

CURRAH: What do they call you now?

　　　　Beat.

RONNIE: The thing is people do call me Mama.

Mama Ronnie.

'Cause I'm like a mother—

I want to look after you—

I'd like you to rely on me—

Do you think you could learn to rely on me?

CURRAH: Dunno. Maybe.

RONNIE: Wonderful!

[*To* TYRELLE] She never had a mother really, you see.

TYRELLE: [*dry*] I know, Ronnie—I read the stories.

RONNIE: I think what was so fascinating—look, all that stuff about your mother was fascinating, it was—and terribly sad that she died— terribly terribly sad, especially so young—but what fascinated me— and really you only touched on it—is, well—your father.

CURRAH: My father?

RONNIE: Yes. And the cellar. The cellar.

I mean—incredible. The cellar.

CURRAH: My cellar?

RONNIE: Let's not talk about it—really—let's not.

It's so depressing.

TYRELLE: It is. It's awful.

RONNIE: And she lived it.

TYRELLE: I don't know how you coped—I really don't.

I mean you didn't even really talk about it—

So much as just alluded to it—

What went on down there—

It makes my skin crawl really—

Look—my skin's crawling!

And you didn't even say what it was—

RONNIE: It must be so upsetting to talk about.

Let's not talk about it anymore—

You've already lived it—and now you write about it.

Or at least, allude to it in your writing. It's too much.

Let's not talk about it anymore, it's just too depressing.

> *Beat.*

Yet so interesting.

> *Beat.*

What happened in the cellar?

Beat.

MIRI *sizes this up. It's another big moment.*

And then she jumps.

CURRAH: You can imagine.

RONNIE: Yes. I can.

Awful.

CURRAH: I don't want to talk about it.

RONNIE: Course not.

Course not.

So upsetting. Really upsetting.

Especially if it's as bad as I imagine it…

CURRAH: Oh, it's not so bad—

RONNIE: No?

CURRAH: I enjoyed it.

RONNIE: Enjoyed it?

TYRELLE: Oh, my God!

CURRAH: I did—I couldn't help it—

RONNIE: Sweet Jesus—

I can't think about it anymore—

But you enjoyed it a lot?

CURRAH: Terribly.

TYRELLE: Didn't it hurt?

CURRAH: Sometimes—

RONNIE: It hurt a lot?

CURRAH: Of course it did. Sometimes.

RONNIE: Of course it hurt—what was I thinking—

Beat.

Did you enjoy the hurt an *awful* lot?

CURRAH: I never wanted it to stop.

Beat.

RONNIE: Oh. Darling.

Poor, poor darling.

TYRELLE: Poor, sweet, darling little Currah.

And to think you survived.

RONNIE: Not only survived.

Lived to tell the tale.

TYRELLE: So it can never happen again.

RONNIE: That's right.

Never happen again.

Currah?

Beat.

CURRAH: It can't ever happen again.

RONNIE: We'll get you counselling—

(We'll get someone to tape them—)

CURRAH: I don't need counselling.

RONNIE: Course you don't.

CURRAH: I don't.

RONNIE: And I'm agreeing.

What you need is *my* representation!

Beat.

CURRAH: I don't know.

RONNIE: We haven't spent the last three months talking on email for nothing, have we?

CURRAH: I guess—

RONNIE: See, Currah—someone with your—talents—well—I can understand it's an exciting time and there must be a lot of people promising the world and it's all very heady and frightening. But let me be your guard dog.

CURRAH: Um—I can't—

RONNIE: Just say it—

CURRAH: I can't—I need—

RONNIE: Say whatever it is you're thinking—

TYRELLE: Say it!

RONNIE: Pop it out!

Beat.

CURRAH: I need to chuck a piss.

RONNIE: Well, maybe it's best you go do that, then.

    CURRAH *walks into the bathroom*

[*To* TYRELLE, *sotto voce*] She's good.

TYRELLE: She's brilliant.

    You know what she's like?

RONNIE: She's like—butter.

TYRELLE: That's right—soft creamy whippery steaming hot butter!

RONNIE: And that gorgeous woebegone face.

    My God.

    The story would sell no matter what—let's face it—it's interesting—

    But the fact that she's Aboriginal—

TYRELLE & RONNIE: [*together*] GOLD!

RONNIE: Marketing fucking Gold.

TYRELLE: Some god just shat you down a little piece of abused heaven.

RONNIE: She's like Fritzl.

TYRELLE: Indigenous Fritzl.

RONNIE: And she liked it—?

TYRELLE: I know she liked it—?

RONNIE: I can't imagine liking it—

TYRELLE: But I want to hear more about her liking it—

RONNIE: Me too—me too—

    It's very common, so I've read—they always like it—

TYRELLE: Mmm—well, I had a boyfriend who used to slap my ass while
    he was doing me and I liked that—

RONNIE: Mmm, yes—I used to like that too—

    Do you think she could do 'Sunrise'?

TYRELLE: Darling, I think she would crucify 'Sunrise'.

RONNIE: Yes. I can imagine her on 'Sunrise'.

TYRELLE: Bawling her little eyes out.

RONNIE: Snot flying everywhere.

TYRELLE: Gut-wrenching sobs of pain and reflection and redemption.

RONNIE: Think of the bored housewives.

TYRELLE: Crying into their cornflakes.

RONNIE: Think of the sales.

TYRELLE: Everyone out there crying.

Crying over our Currah.

CURRAH re-emerges.

RONNIE: Currah—just so you know I'm serious—

I showed a publisher friend your stories—he loved them—I knew he would—

She takes out a manila folder.

Here's a contract for your first book, to be called *Nobody's Girl*— I think you'll find the offer exceedingly generous for an unpublished writer…

She slides the manila folder across.

CURRAH picks it up and scans—she sees the figure.

She gasps and puts it back down.

CURRAH: You not shitting, are you?

RONNIE: I never 'shit' about the important things.

CURRAH: And I get that—

If I just have to write a little book—

RONNIE: Oh, yes.

You just have to talk about your father more—about what happened in the cellar—

What do you say?

CURRAH: Fuck, yes.

ANTHONY knocks at the door.

ANTHONY: [*off*] Are you ready?

She'll be here in a second—

CURRAH: Anthony—

Hold on—the door—

She opens it.

ANTHONY: Oh good, you're / all ready, Miri—

CURRAH: They're here!

ANTHONY: They're here?

Who's they?

TYRELLE: Tyrelle—Ronnie's assistant—

RONNIE: I'm Ronnie—Currah's *agent*—

ANTHONY: Her agent?

RONNIE: That's right—her *agent*.

ANTHONY: I can't believe I'm finally meeting you.

RONNIE: Yes, well.

I think we all owe you a debt of gratitude Anthony (it is Anthony, isn't it?)

Beat.

ANTHONY: My name is Ant.

RONNIE: (I thought—Anthony?)

ANTHONY: All my friends call me Ant—

TYRELLE: Oh, Ant. Yes.

It's so much more—contemporary.

RONNIE: Edgy even.

TYRELLE: Mmm.

ANTHONY: But what's this—Currah—she's your *agent*?

RONNIE: Currah has agreed to be represented by me.

ANTHONY: She has?

RONNIE: Yes.

ANTHONY: Currah, surely you should have talked with me first—

RONNIE: Really—

ANTHONY: [*conspiratorially*] To be honest—I—I—well, there is other interest—and I get, well, worried about her—she can be very sensitive—she needs a lot of protection, I'm sure you can understand—

RONNIE: And that's what I'm here to provide—

ANTHONY: Well, to be honest—she needs the protection by the people that already know her—that care for her best interests.

RONNIE: Are you saying I don't?

ANTHONY: I'm just saying that Currah should consult with the person she already has a trusted relationship with…

RONNIE: Oh look, Currah. You've found your very own bleeding heart.

Beat.

ANTHONY: I think maybe we—got off on the wrong—

    What I mean is—

    I found her—I helped her—she trusts me—

    I told her to write her stories down—as therapy—at night when she got lonely I was the one she'd call—

    Beat.

CURRAH: I did—that's what I did alright—

RONNIE: Thank God for Anthony.

ANTHONY: Ant.

RONNIE: Ant. Thank God for Ant!

ANTHONY: Yes.

TYRELLE: Thank God for Ant!

ANTHONY: Thank you.

CURRAH: Ant. They're going to publish my book—

    Wait till you see how much!

RONNIE: It's going to be marvellous.

    Currah's going to tell us all about what went on the cellar.

ANTHONY: You—what?

CURRAH: I just have to talk about my dad more…

ANTHONY: Hold on—

RONNIE: Everyone wants to know…

    Beat.

ANTHONY: Have you signed something?

CURRAH: No—

ANTHONY: She's not doing anything without *my* approval—

RONNIE: Your—*approval?*

ANTHONY: She needs me—

RONNIE: I'm sure she does—

CURRAH: Anthony—

ANTHONY: Ant—

CURRAH: Ant—I want to—

ANTHONY: It's *my* decision—

RONNIE: Well, actually no—it's *Currah's* decision—

ANTHONY: I won't let her be taken advantage of—

RONNIE: And if she decides to sign—she can sign—

>   *Beat.*

ANTHONY: No she can't.

CURRAH: I can't?

RONNIE: And *why* is that?

ANTHONY: I have POA.

RONNIE: POA?

ANTHONY: Yes. POA.

RONNIE: What the fuck is POA?

ANTHONY: Power of Attorney.

>   POA.

RONNIE: Power of Attorney? Currah?

ANTHONY: We agreed her giving me POA is the best way to ensure she doesn't fall into anything—willy-nilly—

>   That's why she gave me POA.

RONNIE: Will you stop saying POA.

>   This isn't 'Law and fucking Order'.

>   Currah—why didn't you mention you'd given this—*Ant*—Power of Attorney?

CURRAH: For God sake, Ant—read what it says—

>   CURRAH *hands him the contract.*

>   *He takes it and—slowly—reads it.*

ANTHONY: You *require* that she *explicitly* go into detail over the business in the cellar—

RONNIE: [*terse*] Yes.

ANTHONY: Why do you care so much about the cellar?

RONNIE: We're giving the public what they want.

ANTHONY: I don't think you understand—her stories have been— they're about her struggle to fit into the world—to make something of herself—to deal with her self—hatred—

RONNIE: Yes, a nice little misery memoir

ANTHONY: She doesn't write memoir—she writes stories based on her memories of certain events.

RONNIE: It's the same thing.

ANTHONY: It's not.

RONNIE: People aren't interested in stories. They're interested in the truth.

ANTHONY: But what if it isn't true?

RONNIE: No-one cares, as long as they say it's true.

ANTHONY: I don't agree with that.

RONNIE: It's the *truth*. People want the *truth*.

CURRAH: [*joking: A Few Good Men*] 'You can't handle the truth!'

> *Beat.*

> *They look at* CURRAH *strangely.*

RONNIE: Listen—this is the sticky end—I know it's never comfortable talking about market practicalities but I know this business. The only difference between fact and fiction is the way you package it.

Currah needs to consolidate. She has an opportunity.

ANTHONY: You people want to fetishise her life.

RONNIE: We want to celebrate her life!

ANTHONY: Her father raped her in a cellar—

And you want the dirty details—

RONNIE: It would heal her.

ANTHONY: By airing all her dirty laundry?

RONNIE: The truth is always redemptive.

ANTHONY: There is nothing redemptive talking about your father fucking you.

RONNIE: There is everything redemptive talking about your father fucking you!

Currah's story needs to be packaged as a memoir or this exceedingly generous deal will disappear entirely.

ANTHONY: No. I just can't approve of this—

RONNIE: You want her to lose any chance of making some money?

ANTHONY: I know what's best for her.

RONNIE: I don't think so—I know what's best for her—

CURRAH: Um—hello—I'm actually right here, you know.

> *Beat.*

ANTHONY: I'm here too.

RONNIE: And I'm very much here.

>*Beat.*

TYRELLE: Yes—well—I don't think you've actually heard me here in this conversation—excuse me but I haven't been heard.

>*Beat.*

I need a drink.

RONNIE: Of course—course—great idea.

Let's have a drink—take our minds off it—have a momie!

I was going to save this for after the signature but you know what they all say—

A drink helps the think!

>RONNIE *pulls out champagne.*

TYRELLE: Oh nice, Ronnie—

CURRAH: What's that—?

RONNIE: Champagne, love—

>RONNIE *takes off the packaging and pops the cork.*

CURRAH: Champagne?

RONNIE: That's right, darling—for you—

Nothing makes me happier than champagne—

(Except a little signature…)

Let's drink while we think, yes?

>*They all nod to each other and take a sip.*

>*Beat.*

Oh shit, it's warm. How can it be warm?

TYRELLE: You brought us warm champagne?

RONNIE: Of course I didn't—do I look like a fucking imbecile?

I hate that—you buy a bottle—you pay an absolute fortune—I mean you know what I mean—

TYRELLE: Oh yes—I understand.

RONNIE: And the bottle feels cold—it's cold—it's got condescension— condescension?

ANTHONY: Condensation—

RONNIE: Yes condensation, you think the fucker's cold and you open it up
and it tastes like—like—and really you think—why do I bother—why
don't I just fizz up some cat's piss and drink that?!

I'm so sorry, Currah, you were meant to drink ice-cold champagne—
ice-cold.

> *Beat.*

TYRELLE: The hotel surely must have ice.

ANTHONY: Yes, at reception.

RONNIE: Thank you.

ANTHONY: What?

RONNIE: For offering to go to reception.

ANTHONY: I—

RONNIE: What a darling you are.

TYRELLE: That is so nice of you.

ANTHONY: But—

RONNIE: [*to* CURRAH] You're so lucky to have found him.

ANTHONY: Currah, why don't you go?

CURRAH: I don't want to go.

ANTHONY: Currah, go and get us some ice.

RONNIE: You're making your *client* get you ice?

TYRELLE: Does she soak your feet at night as well?

ANTHONY: What?

TYRELLE: Get on her knees and *anoint* your baby Jesus?

RONNIE: So where *actually* are you staying? Not in this room, I hope…

TYRELLE: Oh my, what would the Department of Social Services say…?

> *Beat.*

ANTHONY: I'll be right back.

RONNIE: He's a sweetheart—

TYRELLE: You're very lucky—

> ANTHONY *has left.*

RONNIE: You've got to get rid of him—

TYRELLE: He's awful!

RONNIE: Awful!

Currah—listen to me—

Get rid of the social worker.

Get a fag instead—they do the same thing as a social worker but their drugs are much, much better.

TYRELLE: Mm-hmm.

RONNIE: That man's an idiot, darling—he doesn't know what he's talking about—a Power of Attorney doesn't stop you from signing your own name—It's perfectly legal if you sign for yourself…

TYRELLE: She's right, you know. I've dated lawyers.

RONNIE: You make your own decision—

Don't be influenced by him—

Do what's best for you—

CURRAH: I don't know…

RONNIE: Don't you want a publishing contract?

Pick up the pen, honey.

Just sign.

CURRAH *picks up the pen. Is about to sign.*

ANTHONY *walks in holding a bucket of ice.*

ANTHONY: There was a machine on the floor—

What are you doing?

Beat.

CURRAH: I can still sign for myself, Ant. You can't stop me.

A POA doesn't mean you can stop me…

Beat.

ANTHONY *is thinking fast.*

ANTHONY: I didn't want to say this—I really didn't—but I'm not just her POA—that's not the full picture. You see with Currah's history of abuse she hasn't always had the capacity to make positive life choices—she's been vulnerable to—*exploitation*—and I'm here to make sure that doesn't happen again. That's why I was appointed her guardian—her enduring guardian—so she can't enter into contracts that might—do her harm.

RONNIE: And you have proof of this—?

ANTHONY: I'll send you the documentation tomorrow…

CURRAH: Please, Ant—I don't know what the big deal is—

Just sign. I want you to.

It won't mean I'm exploited.

It means I get a lot of money. I get a book.

I get my name in the papers.

RONNIE: She would get a lot of publicity.

CURRAH: And everyone will know that you helped me—

That you were the one that saved me.

Please, Ant.

She moves to him—looks up with eager eyes.

Beat.

ANTHONY: [*to* CURRAH] You want me to do this?

CURRAH: For both of us.

ANTHONY: How can I say no to that…?

RONNIE pushes the contract and a pen across to ANTHONY.

He picks up the pen and is about to sign but…

CURRAH: One more thing—

RONNIE: [*irritated*] What?

ANTHONY: What?

CURRAH: I was scared to write that I enjoyed it—

But if I'm going to do this book—I have to write about how I enjoyed it and you're not allowed to change it—

ANTHONY: But you didn't enjoy it!

CURRAH: I did too! I just felt too ashamed to say it.

But I did—and what's more—I miss it!

RONNIE: Currah!

TYRELLE: Sweet precious baby—it's not good to miss it.

CURRAH: Well I do, and that's the truth and unless I can say it I'm not writing the book—

ANTHONY: You can't say that.

RONNIE: She's already had one bad father, she doesn't need another!

You can do what you like, Currah—just tell the truth and the people will love you.

Now sign the paper.

ANTHONY: Currah?

CURRAH: Please just sign it, Ant!

For the both of us.

She gives him more wide eyes.

He signs the contact.

RONNIE: All done.

TYRELLE: How does it feel to sell your soul to the devil—haha.

RONNIE: Haha.

ANTHONY: Haha.

CURRAH *puts ice cubes into everyone's champagne—the other three aren't impressed.*

CURRAH: To my new career!

RONNIE: To your new career!

TYRELLE: [*simultaneous*] Your career!

ANTHONY: [*simultaneous, resentful*] Career.

RONNIE: Bad things happen for a reason—that's what my therapist says—

Bad things are just opportunities not yet found.

I think an opportunity just landed on your lap.

She has a sip of champagne before...

We've gotta run.

Off to a reading.

TYRELLE: Oh, that stupid fucking food memoir.

RONNIE: If I have to listen to one more person find redemption from the perfect bouillabaisse I'm going to scream.

TYRELLE: People will pay for anything these days.

RONNIE: Currah, it was lovely to meet you. Really it was.

They are at the door.

CURRAH: Thank you.

ANTHONY *holds out his hand to shake.*

ANTHONY: Good to meet you.

> RONNIE *looks at him, then back to* CURRAH.

RONNIE: Don't be a stranger—call any time.
Let's talk soon, darling—Remember I'm here for you—I love you—I
want to support you—that's my job okay, honey, my job, yes?
That's your cue to say something grateful, Currah!

> *Beat.*

CURRAH: Thanks.

RONNIE: You darling!
Oh, and Currah?

CURRAH: Yes?

RONNIE: Welcome to the family.

> *She kisses* CURRAH *on the cheek and is off with* TYRELLE.

> ANTHONY *shuts the door.*

> MIRI *looks to* ANTHONY *uncertainly.*

> *He can't stop staring at her.*

MIRI: What—what?
Did I do good?

> *Beat.*

ANTHONY: You were terrifying.

> *Beat.*

MIRI: So you got yourself a big fancypants book to write—
ANTHONY: And looks like I'll be needing you again—
MIRI: Looks like it—

> MIRI *smiles.*

SCENE TWO

One year later.

RONNIE *appears on a female talk show.*

RONNIE: This memoir, *Nobody's Girl*—it's a game changer.
There's a section where she describes what it was like being locked

in the cellar—and she writes about it with such—I said, 'Currah—
you can't say that?!' But thank God she has.

[*Reading*] 'It smells like the dark and it feels like the night and even
if I'm lying there alone the air is thick and warm and comforting
like Dad's cigarette breath steaming up the back of my neck. He'd
call me Sugar, his brown sugar, sweeter on the tongue and all so
tastier than plain sugar, white sugar.' And look I'm not going to read
the next bit on television—you'll have to buy the book…

This girl learned to read by staring at the printed version of *Interview
with a Vampire* while the audio book played. She'd keep listening
on repeat until she could recognise the words!

[*Reading*] 'After we were done—he'd hold me, love me, and he'd
whisper—"You'll never leave me, will you Sugar?" I'll never leave
you, Dad, I'll never stop loving. What he didn't say is he'd leave
me. Crying into a cheap foam mattress trying to breathe in the last
of his scent. He made me his and then cast me adrift. And now I'm
Nobody's Girl.'

Inspirational. In stores next week.

♦ ♦ ♦ ♦ ♦

A better hotel room, with conference facilities attached.

MIRI *is in a bizarre new outfit that is simultaneously grungy, sexy, a tad
trashy and inspired by Aboriginal culture (think dot painting with a touch
of sexy Qantas).*

ANTHONY *sits to one side in a very dark mood.*

CURRAH *is finishing off a practice of her pre-written speech.*

There is clearly a lot *of tension between them.*

CURRAH: [*reading*] 'Before I take my shower in the morning I call him—
and he's the last person I speak to before my head hits the pillow.
When I know that I am shy and awkward and stupid he reminds me I
am confidant and pretty and smart. This world is so hard. But finding
someone you can believe in means you are no longer lonely.'

MIRI *closes her eyes—and holds her belly—an attack of nausea.*

A knock on the door.

TYRELLE: [*offstage*] Vivian?

TYRELLE *honks a mini horn. As well as carrying a large bouquet of flowers, an operatic score blasts from his smart phone.*

CURRAH: What?

TYRELLE: Vivian?

Another honk.

CURRAH: She's not here!

TYRELLE: [*Pretty Woman*] 'PRINCESS VIVIAN!'

CURRAH: I'm not fucking Vivian!

TYRELLE: 'COME DOWN!'

CURRAH *opens the door.*

CURRAH: I don't know who you're talking about—I'm not fucking—Oh—

TYRELLE: 'It had to be the top floor right?'

CURRAH: It's only the second—

TYRELLE: 'Alright, I'm coming up'

He storms into the room, gets on one knee and presents the flowers.

'So what happened after he climbs up the tower and rescues her?'

CURRAH: 'She rescues him right back'?

Cue swelling music as TYRELLE *grabs* CURRAH *and swings her around.*

He is almost crying.

ANTHONY: She's a prostitute, you know.

TYRELLE *breaks away, holds* CURRAH'*s hand and looks at* ANTHONY.

TYRELLE: It's the only way I know how to love…

CURRAH: 'I never treated you as a prostitute.'

TYRELLE: 'You just did.'

LMAO. Totes. Amaze. Fuck me bareback.

CURRAH: They're so beautiful—

TYRELLE: I can't believe it's been a year—I wanted to—you know—Congratufuckulations—

CURRAH: They're amazing.

They really are—

TYRELLE: Oh, stop—as if you're not used to flowers by now—

CURRAH: No—I've never gotten flowers.

    TYRELLE *screams.*

TYRELLE: That is a crime against humanity!

    ROFL. Sorry I'm late.

    Cab drivers. If they're not trying to punch you they're trying to fuck you—haha.

CURRAH: It's fine—totally—

TYRELLE: Seriously—I fucking hate racist transphobic homophobic towel heads I really do—

CURRAH: Yeah, they suck—

TYRELLE: He better not sue! At least he wasn't hurt.

    Well, a bit of a bloody nose but I'm sure they can reset it—

    Anyhow, what the fuck—look at you!

    What the fuck?!

CURRAH: You like it?

TYRELLE: I LOVE IT!

CURRAH: You don't think I look like a tramp?

    He thinks I look like a tramp.

TYRELLE: No! Yes!

    But I love it. Sordid heroin chic goes walkabout. Yummy!

    I hadn't seen that one—

    I saw a couple of the other ones they were talking about and I was like, uh-uh.

CURRAH: There were other dresses?

TYRELLE: I wouldn't call 'em dresses—

    If I see one more Indigi girl in a floral print I will not be blamed for the genocide…

    So. How now brown cow?

    Harper's fucking Bazaar.

CURRAH: 'Watch this Talent'.

TYRELLE: Did you enjoy the photo shoot?

    The photographer's hot, right—?

CURRAH: Yeah, he was hot.

TYRELLE: He didn't touch you? Sometimes he likes to have a bit of a touch.

CURRAH: No.

TYRELLE: How you feeling?

CURRAH: You know—

TYRELLE: Mmm-hmm.

CURRAH: I've never spoken in front of people before…

TYRELLE: If anyone tells you to imagine everyone naked—*don't do it!* It's very distracting.

Should we start?

CURRAH: Sure—

TYRELLE *begins to record the interview.*

TYRELLE: In the last two months you have been getting a shitload of buzz.

What is the one piece of advice you'd like to give to aspiring abuse victims interested in telling their stories?

Beat.

MIRI *looks to* ANTHONY. *He doesn't look at her.*

CURRAH: Um. Well—I don't really know…

TYRELLE: Oh. Well, let me—picture this—a kid is out there—struggling—suicidal—about to jump—what do you whisper in their ear?

Again MIRI *looks to* ANTHONY. *He's not playing ball.*

CURRAH: It gets better.

TYRELLE: Mm. Okay—it's been done—you got more?

Beat.

CURRAH: Anthony?

ANTHONY: Mm?

CURRAH: Whadda you reckon?

TYRELLE: It's your interview, baby—

ANTHONY: It's your interview, baby—

TYRELLE: Yeah—who cares about the social worker, right?

So, Currah—just tell me—what do you want people to say about you?

Beat.

CURRAH: She's really hot.

TYRELLE: That's cool, sweetheart—course—we'll come back to that one—

So—look well—easy question—today's the big day—your first public appearance, tell us how you've prepared.

　　CURRAH *shrugs.*

Work with me—

Which day spa did you go to?

CURRAH: The one here at the hotel—dunno the name—

TYRELLE: It's fine—I'll look it up—good—great—

So what's your hair-care routine?

CURRAH: Um. Well—um, I guess every coupla days I use Pears Two in One.

TYRELLE: Okay. Sure. I can go with that.

To remember where you're from right…

And then as a treat you use a deluxe Moroccanoil steam infusion.

CURRAH: Yeah, totally—

TYRELLE: Okay okay okay, so let's—change direction— (sheesh—)

You said this will be the first time you've ever speak'd in public.

How have you prepared—

CURRAH: Well, I've got my speech—

　　She points to her speech lying on the table.

　　RONNIE *enters, on the phone (it's an earpiece of course).*

RONNIE: She won't stop crying—I don't know why you hired her—

Don't take that tone with me—I had a little word—the teensiest little word—about the lighting (it looks like a fucking mortuary) and she started crying.

Don't scream at me, just fucking fix it!

　　She hangs up and turns towards CURRAH.

Well, there's no doubting you're Aboriginal.

CURRAH: I can be something else.

RONNIE: No. Just please—for my sake—don't go on and on about it in your speech. Except your welcome to country! Don't forget your welcome to country.

CURRAH: It's not my country.

RONNIE: Now now, there's no need to be like that—

We're all Australians, darling.

Now come on—they're wanting to sound check—it's time to come down…

TYRELLE: We're still doing the interview, baby—

TYRELLE *opens his arms for a hug.*

RONNIE: Speaking of subtle—how's the new job going?

TYRELLE: Love it!

RONNIE: So come on, Currah—

TYRELLE: I need her to finish the interview—

RONNIE: I need her to sound check—

TYRELLE: Why can't you do it?

RONNIE: I need someone who's actually speaking…

ANTHONY: I could do it?

Test the sound—I guess—

CURRAH: Fine—just leave me then—

RONNIE*'s phone is ringing furiously—*

RONNIE: Oh alright, come on—let's go—

RONNIE *leaves with* ANTHONY.

TYRELLE *is looking through* CURRAH*'s speech.*

TYRELLE: [*reading*] 'Thanks, Anthony, for those amazing words.'

Who wrote this?!

CURRAH: Me.

TYRELLE: [*reading*] 'God, this is "deadly"—'

Love it.

CURRAH: Saying deadly is so gammon.

TYRELLE: [*reading*] 'He's the last person I speak to before my head hits the pillow…'?

CURRAH: Oh yeah, right…

TYRELLE: [*reading*] 'Finding someone you believe in means you're no longer lonely…'

   Beat.

What the hell is going on?

CURRAH: What?

TYRELLE: Where the hell is Currah?

CURRAH: I am Currah.

TYRELLE: Well, where are you?

CURRAH: I'm just really nervous.

TYRELLE: You're being *weird*.

CURRAH: No I'm not.

TYRELLE: Is it Anthony?

CURRAH: What about him?

TYRELLE: Were you—looking to him for answers?

CURRAH: No!

TYRELLE: Back then?

CURRAH: Course not.

TYRELLE: You're giving me one-word answers.

CURRAH: He just helps coach me a bit.

TYRELLE: Can I quote you on that?

CURRAH: No. I mean—fuck—he's just—

TYRELLE: Oh, my God—you've got to get rid of him—

This is so creepy.

> RONNIE *enters—on the phone—holding a bark and/or fruit sculpture that sits so high it somehow precariously defies the laws of gravity.*

RONNIE: I'll be down when I'm down—I'm hurrying, alright—

[*To* CURRAH] I never give flowers so don't get used to this but—congratulations.

You know the first time you become published is a lot like the first time you make love with a man…

She hasn't thought this piece of wisdom out so carefully…

[*Correcting*] Err, well, I mean—

TYRELLE: [*sympathetic to* RONNIE*'s plight*] Oh, Ronnie.

RONNIE: Anyway, congratulations, my dear.

She hands over the flowers.

CURRAH: They must have cost a fortune.

RONNIE: Oh, a little second mortgage—

TYRELLE: You've got to tell her—

CURRAH: Please don't.

RONNIE: Tell me what?

TYRELLE: There's a problem.

CURRAH: Tyrelle!

RONNIE: Oh?

CURRAH: It's nothing.

TYRELLE: It's not nothing.

RONNIE: Currah?

Beat.

CURRAH: It's Anthony.

RONNIE: Oh, you should hear him down there—

TYRELLE: Wait till you hear what he's done—

CURRAH: He hasn't done anything—

TYRELLE: Oh, he has…

RONNIE: What's the problem?

Beat.

Spit it out.

TYRELLE: He's been—'interfering'.

RONNIE: He touched you?

TYRELLE: No.

RONNIE: What?

CURRAH: He's just been helping coach me.

TYRELLE: Something weird is going on—it's like he's been telling her
    what to say—

CURRAH: He's just been helping me—

RONNIE: Is this true, Currah?

CURRAH: Just a little bit—

RONNIE: He's trying to put words in your mouth?

CURRAH: He won't do that anymore.

RONNIE: He certainly won't.

And he won't be introducing you either!

CURRAH: No, but he's got to—

RONNIE: Over my dead body.

I trust you'll be discreet about this, Tyrelle, remember who got you the job!

We'll get that stupid child abuse woman—Vicki—you know—runs the charity—

Bah, can't remember—she'd love to introduce you I'm sure—

CURRAH: Really?

RONNIE: I'll go check—

CURRAH: I can't do this, Ronnie—

RONNIE: What do you mean?

CURRAH: I wanna be sick.

RONNIE: Currah—I have to go be nice to people I'd rather spit at—I don't need this right now.

When in doubt, be amazing—it's always worked for me—

[*On the phone*] Is that stupid Vicki woman—child abuse charity— still propping up the bar—?

RONNIE *has left.*

CURRAH: I want to throw up.

TYRELLE: Do you want me to hold your hair?

CURRAH: Who do I think I am?

I'm no-one.

TYRELLE: Oh no, honey—

CURRAH: I am. I'm no-one.

TYRELLE: You stop that now—

CURRAH: They're all—fancy—they've got education—

They're gonna think I'm a fraud—

TYRELLE: Stop that right fucking now!

Hell's bells no!

You're Currah—nothing more, nothing less.

And that is amazing, you hear—you're just *you!*

And to hear you stymie yourself 'cause of some douche bag—

And now you doubt yourself because of some stupid pretentious literary fuckers...

Oh shit—here it comes—this is going to be ugly—oh God—

FUCK NO!

It's just—my—my—anger—

See, people think I'm less than them—because—I'm—I'm—

Black, you know—and *outré*—

Camp. Fucking camp fucking black row of fucking tents.

And it's why I can't get a boyfriend

> RONNIE *enters—a woman on a mission. She goes to a drawer—rummages for painkillers—swallows two dry—slams the drawer shut—and walks out without a word.*

And I'm just so tired of men using me just for sex—and chewing me up—and why do I never get a plus-one at a wedding? And why does the best man's friend with the hot wife always proposition me in the toilets? And why do those towel head cabbies want to have sex with me—and still expect me to pay my fare?

Like I'm some—some—handmaiden whore.

CURRAH: Handmaiden whore?

TYRELLE: And I don't really talk to my folks—'cause—well—they thought I should—you know—

Go into construction.

Can you imagine me in construction?

But I'm here—and I'm reporting (whoopdee fuck) and my life is supposedly fine and I've gotten here myself and I'm so fucking angry at everyone that I want to kill taxi drivers—

Because I used to fuck taxi drivers when I couldn't afford the fare.

And now they still expect me to pay as well!

And you—you've been locked in a cellar—

Your father raped you—

You *enjoyed* it!

(I didn't mind the cab drivers, it must be said...)

And you're here, telling us all about it and you don't feel shame—or guilt—or rage.

And all I do is feel shame and guilt and rage.

And now you're saying you care about some privileged fucks?

That you'll listen to what some douche bag wants you to say?

No. That makes me want to pull out a gun and shoot someone.

Because if you can't be amazing then who can?

It's like I'll never be anything but a—a—

Camp Black Faggot.

> TYRELLE *sobs.*

> *Beat.*

CURRAH: Tyrelle—no—please—

Come here—

TYRELLE: A camp black faggot...

CURRAH: No...

> *She rests* TYRELLE's *head on her boob and tentatively strokes his head.*

> *A beat. And then—spur of the moment—she begins to sing the first chorus of 'Edelweiss', from* The Sound of Music.

> TYRELLE *is initially surprised, until he joins in to finish off the chorus in harmony.*

CURRAH: My father used to sing that to me after he'd—you know.

TYRELLE: Really?

CURRAH: Really.

And it always made me feel good.

> *Beat.*

TYRELLE: You get it.

CURRAH: I do?

TYRELLE: Being black—being—well—you know—different.

CURRAH: Yeah.

> *Beat.*

TYRELLE: That ole chestnut!

CURRAH: No-one wants to talk about it, do they?

TYRELLE: No-one wants to *stop* talking about it these days.

CURRAH: Yeah, I know. It's so cliché.

TYRELLE: You—you tell it like it is.

> *Beat.*

CURRAH: I'd rather be back in the cellar.
At least in the cellar there's something to believe in.

TYRELLE: Believe in?

CURRAH: Maybe next time he'd tell me he loves me while he's—

> *Beat.*

TYRELLE: Oh my—fuck—
You're so—

CURRAH: I'm just me…

TYRELLE: Sometimes—I just wanna—well—

CURRAH: What?

TYRELLE: Scream.

CURRAH: Me too.

TYRELLE: Stupid fucking camp black queenie faggot.

CURRAH: Do it.

TYRELLE: What?

CURRAH: Scream it!

TYRELLE: I can't.

CURRAH: Scream it!

TYRELLE: I am not a racist or homo or transphobic person!

CURRAH: Scream it!

TYRELLE: I love my difference.

CURRAH: Scream it!

TYRELLE: I love myself.

CURRAH: SCREAM IT!

TYRELLE: STUPID FUCKING CAMP BLACK QUEENIE FAGGOT!

CURRAH: YOU STUPID FUCKING CAMP BLACK QUEENIE FAGGOT!

TYRELLE: I AM!
I'M A STUPID FUCKING CAMP BLACK QUEENIE FAGGOT.

[*Surprised*] It feels so good.

CURRAH: So did my father fucking me.

> *Beat.*

> TYRELLE *bursts into giggles.*

TYRELLE: You've got to stop saying that!

CURRAH: You should try it, Tyrelle. Get some rich white daddy to treat you mean.

TYRELLE: There's my interview!

CURRAH: Really?

TYRELLE: You are so special. You're the most special one of all.

> RONNIE *re-enters.*

CURRAH. [*screaming*] STUPID FUCKING CAMP BLACK QUEENIE FAGGOT!

RONNIE: [*on the phone*] Is she ready… Yes I'm checking.

[*To* CURRAH] So *is* she ready?

CURRAH: Fuck no!

RONNIE: [*on the phone*] Yes—she's dressed and ready—

[*Eyeing* CURRAH, *on the phone*] Haha—'Stranded in the outback and oops my underwear fell off.'

> *She hangs up.*

[*To* CURRAH] Sweetheart, it's all sorted. That woman'll introduce you. She cried when I asked her. Silly drunk.

Oh, and Bryce Courtney just walked in the door—

CURRAH: Fuck—where's Anthony—I need Anthony—

> RONNIE*'s phone rings—she looks at the ID.*

RONNIE: Finally!

And this, baby girl, is your future on the line…

[*Answering*] Darling?

I thought you'd become afraid of me…

Too big? Bullshit! No-one else has her authenticity, she's gonna be a hit, I promise you…

> RONNIE *exits the room.*

TYRELLE: I haven't seen her like this for *years*.

CURRAH: Really?

TYRELLE: [*vicious gossip*] You know what they've been calling her?

CURRAH: What?

TYRELLE: You can't tell anyone—

CURRAH: I won't.

TYRELLE: Shit Mama.

CURRAH: Shit Mama?

TYRELLE: She ain't been Midas for a while...

Don't tell her I said that.

CURRAH: I won't.

> RONNIE *re-enters.*

RONNIE: [*on the phone*] No—I'm not going to—listen—

You are a grain of sand in the beach of my fucking career!

> *She hangs up.*

Fucking bull dyke stage managers.

Tyrelle—I love you et cetera but it's time to go.

TYRELLE: I'll see you downstairs—you're gonna be amazing.

> *Over his shoulder...*

Stupid fucking camp black queenie faggot!

> CURRAH *smiles.*

RONNIE: Quickly, darling—just quickly—so glad you spoke with me before about all that—it's been in my head for quite some time—this Anthony situation—can I be frank?

> *Beat.*

I don't get it.

I've done as you asked—I accepted him signing for you—even if it turns my stomach but you insisted—

CURRAH: I know—

RONNIE: I deposit the money into his account—I presume he's paying you correctly—you got the money I sent through today—

CURRAH: Yes, absolutely.

RONNIE: You're so strong and sassy and defiant with everyone else.

But with him you turn into a cloying little girl—

CURRAH: I have to be on stage in a minute—

RONNIE: Are you having sex with him?

CURRAH: No.

RONNIE: You're not?

CURRAH: I'm not.

RONNIE: Then what the hell is he doing here?

>   *Beat.*

CURRAH: He's my social worker—he helped facilitate my recovery and is the one that led me to therapeutic writing.

RONNIE: Yes, I've read the jacket cover.

But you don't need a social worker anymore. I loved my therapist too—and then I realised how much he cost—

CURRAH: Anthony's not in it for the money—

RONNIE: That's what my husband said!

Honey—I've watched the interviews—I see how you look to him—who doesn't love a daddy—but listen here—that's for the bedroom—don't let a man tell you what to be.

CURRAH: But I don't know what else to do.

RONNIE: You've got so much personality, Currah—your writing—it's incredible—

Trust yourself—talk like you do in your books—

CURRAH: It's different when I speak.

When I speak I need someone to hold my hand.

RONNIE: I'll hold your hand.

Love. All successful people have to—*let go* of some things along the way.

That's what we do—as successful people.

CURRAH: I know—

RONNIE: Anthony is one of those things that needs to be 'let go'.

Mark my words—you are going to be incredible.

That's why we're going on a book tour.

CURRAH: A book tour?

RONNIE: A little national six-month book tour.

With a possibility of extending internationally.

I locked it in this morning.

CURRAH: How the hell is that going to work?

RONNIE: I'll be there—you talk about your books—sign some copies—have a cry—

It'll be easy.

CURRAH: A tour?!

RONNIE: I promise you, Currah—with the right management this could be *remembered*. Do you know how rare that is?

CURRAH: I just don't wanna—disappoint you.

RONNIE: Darling—let me give you some advice—and this is for free—darling—

This is the only advice I have that's worth anything—

> *Her phone rings, she looks at it.*

Sorry, I have to get this.

[*Answering*] Darling? You have a figure for me? Mm?

Let's talk when you're fucking serious!

> *She hangs up.*

Sorry, where was I?

CURRAH: The only bit of advice you have for me?

RONNIE: Only bit of advice—

Nope, it's gone.

> *Beat.*

CURRAH: I'm just scared. What if I'm not good enough?

RONNIE: You've got one of the highest advances for an unpublished writer I've ever seen, the media are having a field day over you. So I think it might be time to admit that you're good. Very good. Otherwise we wouldn't bother.

> *Beat.*

What is it? You're holding something back.

CURRAH: I don't want to go back—

I can't go back.

RONNIE: Where Currah?

CURRAH: Don't make me go back.

RONNIE: Go back to where?

CURRAH: I don't wanna go back.

RONNIE: No-one's making you go back. You're free now.
It's time, honey. For you to be you.

Her phone rings again.

Fuck the consequences! Never go back!

[*Answering*] Yes?

What do you mean Vicki's throwing up in the toilets?

I told you to cut her off.

Fuck!

CURRAH: Ronnie.

RONNIE: [*on the phone*] We need to find someone else—

CURRAH: Ronnie?

RONNIE: [*on the phone*] Find some old black woman—I don't care just—

CURRAH: RONNIE!

RONNIE: What?

CURRAH: I want Anthony to introduce me.

RONNIE: [*on the phone*] I'll call you back.

She hangs up.

CURRAH: He's got to introduce me.

RONNIE: But we just talked—I thought you agreed—it's your time—

CURRAH: Ronnie!

Do you trust me?

RONNIE: I guess—

CURRAH: Then let him introduce me.

RONNIE: Alright. I'll let him introduce you.

But promise me—never let anyone stamp on your biggest, brightest self.

You don't need him.

ANTHONY *enters, holding a perfectly respectable, if uninspiring, bunch of flowers.*

Promise?

CURRAH *hesitates.*

ANTHONY: Promise what?

They both look up guiltily.

CURRAH: Oh, hey—

RONNIE: Anthony.

ANTHONY: Ant.

RONNIE: Indeed.

ANTHONY: That's some foyer—the people are spilling out onto the footpath!

RONNIE: We should have let them in by now.

ANTHONY: These are for you. Congratulations.

CURRAH: Can you just put them with the others?

ANTHONY: I didn't know so many people were going to be there.

RONNIE: Yes—well.

ANTHONY: I think it sounded really good—

RONNIE: I'm sure you did.

ANTHONY: Hey—if it's alright—can I please speak to Currah alone?

RONNIE: She really can't. It's almost time.

ANTHONY: Please—I *need* to—I *want* to—

RONNIE: And I'm telling you she can't.

CURRAH: It'll be fine, Ronnie. It's only a minute.

RONNIE: Don't forget what you promised…

RONNIE *leaves.*

Beat.

ANTHONY: What did you promise, Ronnie?

MIRI: She made me promise to be brilliant—

ANTHONY: I'm really sorry about before. I shouldn't have done that. I know I've been a pain.

I'm a bit nervous.

MIRI: I know.

ANTHONY: I just—you know—

Some reviews are out…

MIRI: Already?

ANTHONY: The publicist just gave 'em to me—listen…

[*Reading*] 'This debut novel charts a disturbing course—it shines a light into the darkest recesses of our souls and makes us crave the impossible. It's almost like Currah is daring us to hope the bastard father would open that door one more time, such is the beguiling web that she weaves around her readers.'

Beat.

MIRI: Far out.

ANTHONY: And then there's this—

[*Reading*] '*Nobody's Girl* is quite plainly the most explosive book you'll read this year. The writing is vicious, contemporary, alive. Abuse? She loves it! And so do we. Currah is addictively enjoyable. Masterful.'

Beat.

MIRI: She's amazing, you know.

ANTHONY: She's very different.

MIRI: And you wrote her.

ANTHONY: Yep. Now it's your turn to—

MIRI: Yeah.

ANTHONY: Hey—when I introduce you—can I just check this is right—?

MIRI: What?

ANTHONY: [*reading*] 'I'd like to thank the traditional owners of the land—the Gadigal people of the Eora nation, as they are our traditional owners'—

Is that the right—how do you say—clan?

MIRI: Yeah, maybe…

ANTHONY: Oh, and—

[*Reading*] 'I wanted to advise any Indigenous people present that Currah's mother will be mentioned, and she's dead, so I don't want to cause offence to anyone…'

Beat.

MIRI: You never talk about your family.

ANTHONY: There's nothing to say.

MIRI: Is that why you created her?

ANTHONY: It has nothing to do with them.

MIRI: What are they like?

ANTHONY: They're fine.

MIRI: What does that mean?

ANTHONY: They're just good, normal people.

MIRI: Good, normal people?

ANTHONY: Mum crochets doilies. Dad tinkers in the garage.

They have barbeques on Fridays and Dad drinks too much VB.

The only books Mum ever reads are by Anne Rice.

Dad only reads the union newsletter.

We don't see each other very much and when we do we try to like each other but there's not much to say really.

Beat.

You've got your speech?

MIRI: Yes.

ANTHONY: You feel good about it?

MIRI: It's well-written.

ANTHONY: Thanks.

MIRI: I'm glad you're introducing me.

ANTHONY: That's sweet.

MIRI: Make sure you talk about our connection, okay?

ANTHONY: I will.

We're two peas in a pod we are—

MIRI: Both of us overcoming our loneliness and all—

ANTHONY: Yeah—finally someone who understands—

MIRI: And I love you talking about how you saved me.

'Cause I really feel like you have. Saved me.

Beat.

ANTHONY: You're going to be great.

You have this—light. You make her come alive.

That's why I chose you in the first place—

MIRI: I love her too.

ANTHONY: I can see that. I put the money into your account—

I gave you a bonus—

MIRI: You really shouldn't have…

ANTHONY: Well, it's the final payment—

Thank you.

MIRI: Yeah, well—

She's going to keep getting better and better, you know.

ANTHONY: This is when it all starts.

MIRI: I know you're right.

ANTHONY: I've wanted this moment my whole life.

MIRI: I know you have.

ANTHONY: And now you get to live it for me—

MIRI: Yeah, I do.

ANTHONY: So go out there and—you know—crush 'em!

MIRI: [*almost apologising*] Hey, Anthony.

ANTHONY: What?

MIRI: Thanks. For everything.

RONNIE *enters.*

RONNIE: It's about to start—

CURRAH: Fuck, I wanna spew.

RONNIE: When you speak just imagine the entire audience is naked…

ANTHONY: Someone will tell me when I'm meant to go on, right?

RONNIE: Yes, the lady with the mullet.

Are you all ready, Currah?

CURRAH: No.

ANTHONY: Of course you are.

CURRAH: I can't fucking do this!

RONNIE: You can!

CURRAH: I told you—I can't fucken do this!

RONNIE: But you're amazing, Currah.

ANTHONY: You are. You're amazing.

RONNIE: Trust in yourself.

ANTHONY: You know what to say.

CURRAH: I need a moment, Ronnie.

RONNIE: I'll give you a minute. Only one. Bull dyke will kill me otherwise.
   Come on, Anthony—

ANTHONY: Break a leg, Currah. That's what they say—

CURRAH: I don't wanna fucken break a leg…

> *Beat.*

RONNIE: [*to* ANTHONY *while leaving*] Just so you know, if you talk for
   more than two minutes we'll turn the music on…

> RONNIE *leaves with* ANTHONY.
>
> MIRI *is alone.*
>
> *She picks up the speech, looks at it.*
>
> *Contemplates.*
>
> *Panics.*

CURRAH. Oh fuck. Shit Fucken Shitty Fuck.
   My name is Currah.

> MIRI *is in the spotlight now. She is panicking.*

I dunno what to say.
I've got this speech here.
[*Reading*] 'Thanks, Ant, for those amazing words.'
He wanted me to say that.
He wants me to say a lot of things.
You know how long I've dreamt of this.
Standing here in front of you mob—you giving a shit about what I
have to say.
Oh, fuck. I don't know what to say.
I don't know how to be in this fucking, stupid world.
Everyone always saying what they're meant to say—
Some aunty has a baby—Oh, my God, I'm so happy—
Some person up the road dies—Oh, my God, I'm so sad—
Some social worker helps you—Oh, my God, I'm so happy—
WHY WON'T SOMEONE SAY WHAT THEY MEAN?
Life's like a big fucken dick.
It's hard!

Sometimes I wish we'd all just call these fuckers up and tell 'em what we think of 'em…

'No Limp Dicks!'

You see I don't wanna just be something you pick up off the shelves, look at and throw away.

I wanna be remembered.

You see the thing about Ant is—he thinks he's a really nice guy.

But there's something I really think you should know…

CURRAH *smiles.*

The monster is born.

Blackout.

END OF ACT ONE

ACT TWO

SCENE THREE

One year later.

CURRAH *stands onstage in a different dress, finishing off her speech at one of her sold-out book events.*

She is now very comfortable in her skin—it is like she is doing a form of Anthony Robbins life coaching.

CURRAH: Alright yo, it's Currah! Let me hear ya!

I said let me hear ya!

Shut the fuck up! You guys!

I fucking love my people!

So tell me—who here's been reading the papers recently, hey?

Doesn't it make you fucking sick?

Those people—those smarty-arsed people out there that think they're better than us, right?

You want the truth—I'll give you the truth.

Do you want the truth?

Here it is.

My father sexually abused me and I enjoyed it.

No! Damn it you're right you're right—I lied it's not true you're right I didn't enjoy it.

I fucken loved it!

Say something like that and everyone wanna rip you down.

But you know something?

Who needs them when we got each other, right?

That's why I say to each and every one of you—as your best friend— be who you are. I don't care—just don't intentionally hurt someone else (and no—I'm not talking about S&M you filthy buggers you know I love it too).

The one thing I figured out a li'l while ago—and I wanna get real serious now—see, is—I don't believe in shame.

That shit will eat out all your heart and then go for seconds.

Those people out there they want us to feel ashamed and we say to them—SHAME ON YOU!

Shame on Shame. Shame on Shame. 'Cause we got just as much right to exist as everyone else no matter how much we feel like freaky deformed outsiders 'cause we're into weird shit or weird shit's happened to us or we just wish it would!

So be who you are and please, for me, don't give a shit.

◆ ◆ ◆ ◆ ◆

RONNIE *sits in the nicest hotel room of a large country town.*

She is slowly getting through a very large glass of scotch.

She seems shaky, drained.

She is somewhere far away, amusing herself, but sad.

The radio is on—easy listening—the drum beat in the middle of the song...

RONNIE *has a private moment, singing the chorus of Eric Carmen's 'All By Myself', badly.*

The door rattles as CURRAH *makes her way into the room.*

CURRAH *drunkenly calls out to some people...*

CURRAH: Argh, love ya bastards!
   Call me. You got the number.
   I always answer. Always!
   Hah!

     CURRAH *shuts the door.*

RONNIE: You didn't answer when I called.

CURRAH: Oh. Ronnie.

RONNIE: It's eleven thirty.

CURRAH: Woah—eleven thirty—call the fun police!

RONNIE: I wanted to speak with you—

CURRAH: We're speaking now—

RONNIE: No, I needed to talk with you properly...

CURRAH *does the sirens for the fun police.*

So who was it tonight?

CURRAH: Oh, Ronnie—you should have seen 'em —this sweet kid—he was so sweet—his father used to pimp him out to all his mates—he was so grateful—during the signing he was crying and I was crying and then he introduced me to his cousin—and he took me out—and now that—that's a story—

RONNIE: You certainly know how to connect with them, don't you?

CURRAH: It's not that hard—you just have to listen to them—hear them— and tell them they're not stupid for feeling the way they do—

RONNIE: Yes well—

CURRAH: I mean this tour—I had no idea so many people were in so much pain—

RONNIE: [*drily*] Or had so much disposable income—

CURRAH: They were asking when the movie was gonna come out—

RONNIE: Another lot?

CURRAH: I tell ya, Ronnie—we gotta renew the option—it'd go off— who'd ya reckon'd look hot playing me?

RONNIE: I don't know.

CURRAH: Or my dad—shit—who'd play my dad?

Who'd wanna play my dad?

Russell Crowe. Yeah, he'd do it I reckon…

Beat.

Oh, lighten up, Ronnie.

You've got a face like a cat's arse.

RONNIE: Does that make me a sour puss?

CURRAH: Let Currah make it better—

RONNIE: How would Currah make it better?

CURRAH *pours* RONNIE *a very liberal scotch.*

She passes the glass to RONNIE.

You know I really did love you, baby girl?

CURRAH: What?

RONNIE: I dunno—it's stupid. At first I was just doing my job—but then—well—I couldn't help it—I believed—in you!

CURRAH: What are you talking about?

RONNIE: The whole stupid thing.

CURRAH: It's not stupid—everyone believes in me.

RONNIE: It's going to change.

CURRAH: No it's not.

RONNIE: You're so overdue for your next book—when's it coming?—
'Soon,' you say, 'soon'—And all this pressure to—confirm. Who you
are. 'Who's Currah, who's Currah?'

CURRAH: You've had too much to drink—

RONNIE: I've been waiting for you for hours.

CURRAH: I know we get on each other's nerves a bit but that's just 'cause
we spend 24/7 together—we'll soon finish the tour and—and—

RONNIE: And what?

CURRAH: Go to the next phase.

Beat.

RONNIE: Tell me, Currah, please. What *is* the next phase?

The toilet flushes.

CURRAH: Who's in the toilet?

RONNIE: It's all gonna change, baby girl.

Trust Mama.

ANTHONY *emerges from the bathroom.*

CURRAH: Anthony? What are you doing here?

ANTHONY: I wanted to see you both—

CURRAH: Yes—of course—just—well—it's kinda late—

RONNIE: Don't make me call the fun police—

Beat.

CURRAH: Long time no see.

So what's been happening? Too busy to answer emails, hey?

ANTHONY: I didn't much feel like writing.

CURRAH: Yeah well, I missed you, you know—wanted to touch base—

ANTHONY: You seem to be doing quite well without me—

CURRAH: Not so well—I still need my Ant, don't I—?

ANTHONY: Right.

CURRAH: So do you wanna go out? Just us two. Catch up.

It'll be just like old times?

RONNIE: He came to talk to me actually.

CURRAH: What's he got to say to you?

Anthony?

Ant?

Silence.

I totally missed you, you know—

It's just me—I'm—so happy—

I'm making people so happy.

You should see them, Ant—those people they're so *happy*—finally they got someone they can relate to—that speaks like them—thinks like them—that's been through what they've been through but worse and they're so happy.

And we all have you to—[thank]

RONNIE: DROP THE BULLSHIT, MIRI *SMITH*, I KNOW!

MIRI *looks like she's been slapped.*

I know.

You're good—I'll give you that—you haven't dropped for a second. Not one second.

What did you think you were playing at?

MIRI: I dunno—

RONNIE: You dunno? You dunno?

Beat.

So let me get this right—my baby girl is actually a—carer?

MIRI: Yes.

ANTHONY: Her mother is very sick—

RONNIE: And you're from—

MIRI: Down south.

It's a tiny town—

RONNIE: How big?

MIRI: Coupla hundred.

RONNIE: And you look after your sick mother?

MIRI: Yes.

RONNIE: And you're actually a high school dropout—

MIRI: Someone had to look after her—

RONNIE: Are you even Aboriginal?

MIRI: Yes!

RONNIE: Well, that's something.

And let me get this right—you know him—how?

MIRI: He was my mother's case worker for a while—

That's how we met. He called me up one day and offered me some money to do this…

RONNIE: And your dad?

MIRI: Never knew him. He left…

RONNIE: And the rest of your family?

MIRI: Don't know 'em … They're on the West Coast.

RONNIE: And so no-one ever hit you.

MIRI: I got into a fight once with a chick at school.

RONNIE: And you were never molested?

MIRI: There were a bunch of paedos where I grew up…

RONNIE: But none of them molested you?

MIRI: No.

RONNIE: And no family member raped you.

Long, long pause.

MIRI: No.

RONNIE: This is gonna hit the fan!

MIRI: Only if someone tells.

The only three people that know are standing right here.

Beat.

ANTHONY: I'll tell.

MIRI: Why would you tell?

ANTHONY: I think you know.

MIRI: Come on?

ANTHONY: After what you did to me?

MIRI: I didn't do anything to you.

ANTHONY: You humiliated me.

In front of everyone.

The department—my department—

They wanted to know who you were. Who this strange girl was that I'd—fetishised.

All those phone calls—'No limp dicks!'

I had to quit.

MIRI: You're a really good friend, Ant.

ANTHONY: It's not that simple.

My ex-boss called me up yesterday—out of the blue—said he'd been following you—party girl—motivational speaker—pretty extreme.

I think he's feeling a little humiliated too.

They've been asked to confirm your existence. From your publishers.

And then he said something I found pretty interesting.

Maybe I can even have my job back if I tell 'em who you are—

Beat.

You shouldn't have cut me out.

MIRI: What did you want—? You were in the way—

ANTHONY: I just wanted to be included—

MIRI: You were doing it all wrong—you would have made us be discovered—

ANTHONY: I would not—

MIRI: Admit it, Anthony, you weren't very good—

ANTHONY: That's not true—I am good—It's mine—I created it—I created her—and now you've *stolen her from me*—

MIRI: Yeah—just like Currah's mum was *stolen* from her family?

ANTHONY: Yes—but the people who stole Currah's mum were at least trying to do the right thing.

MIRI: You're saying the people who *stole* Currah's mum were better than me?

ANTHONY: Yes!

MIRI: You've got some nerve.

ANTHONY: I created her!

MIRI: I play her!

ANTHONY: I write her!

MIRI: I live her!

ANTHONY: And I live her too!

> *Beat.*

Don't think I won't go public—tell everyone the whole nasty little farce—let everyone see what a horrible little girl you are.

MIRI: You will not take this away from me—I deserve this—I deserve it—I don't have anything—you—you have everything.

ANTHONY: WHAT DO I HAVE?

MIRI: It must be so hard being you—privileged white boy—

ANTHONY: Oh, yes—that's me—all so privileged—

I had to quit my job—they all thought I was sleazebag—Now I have to work in a community centre—I can't get anything published—

Oh, my life is—is—A-OK

MIRI: A-OK? Boo hoo hoo.

Currah is my chance—she's my opportunity—I'm gonna take it—

ANTHONY: No you won't—she's mine.

MIRI: Just because you can't hack it in the real world—

ANTHONY: Everyone loved what I wrote!

MIRI: Because you wrote it as a black chick.

And even then it only took off 'cause I *made* it real.

> *Beat.*

Would you touch him, Ronnie? Come on—I've been around you long enough—would you touch him?

> *Beat.*

RONNIE: I'm staying out of this.

MIRI: Go on, would you touch him?

RONNIE: I don't know—it's about the work—it's got to be about the quality of the work—it always is—

ANTHONY: What?

RONNIE: It's about the work!

ANTHONY: That's such—bullshit.

I submitted to you—I submitted my manuscripts to you so many times—

RONNIE: Do you know how many unsolicited manuscripts come across my desk every year?

ANTHONY: No.

RONNIE: Neither do I!

But it's a hell of a lot!

ANTHONY: *Verge of Oblivion*—a guy—stuck in a dead-end job—wants to be somewhere else—

RONNIE: Truly memorable—

ANTHONY: Alright—so—I—I—I did an S&M erotic novel too—

MIRI: You did what?

ANTHONY: Yeah—bet you didn't know that!

Edge and Desire—a guy—plain office worker by day—

RONNIE: Transforms into sordid sex worker slash hooker slash assassin by night—

Very original...

ANTHONY: No—shut up. Gets abducted. Enjoys it.

RONNIE: Don't worry—we make good use of those manuscripts. We recycle.

ANTHONY: I remember calling you up—speaking to you—

RONNIE: You did?

ANTHONY: You screamed at me—

RONNIE: What did I say?

ANTHONY: 'Who the fuck do you think you are, calling me? I've got more important things to do than speak to nothing nobodies like you!'

RONNIE: [*cutting him off*] 'I coulda had class.'

ANTHONY: What?

RONNIE: [*from On the Waterfront*] 'I coulda had class!'

ANTHONY: I don't get—

RONNIE: 'I coulda been a contender. I coulda been somebody, instead of a bum, which is what I am, let's face it.'

ANTHONY: What are you talking about?

MIRI: (That's funny.)

RONNIE: (Did you like it?)

MIRI: (I loved it.)

ANTHONY: I coulda been a contender!

If someone had just listened to me!

RONNIE: Couldn't we all, babe. Couldn't we all.

Beat.

Anthony.

ANTHONY: Ant.

RONNIE: Ant.

The fact is—some stories are just more—*marketable* than others.

So you're not happy. Who is?

So you feel like an outsider. Who doesn't?

So you want to be loved. Everyone wants to be loved!

But what's your take—your unique selling point? Huh?

Beat.

MIRI: An Aboriginal girl whose father raped her in a cellar. And enjoyed it.

RONNIE: Now that's what I'm talking about!

Beat.

ANTHONY: That was you—that was you guys—I didn't want to do that—

MIRI: I did. And that's what made it work.

Beat.

ANTHONY: I have demands.

MIRI: What kind of demands?

ANTHONY: If you want me to validate your existence—then I have demands.

MIRI: You're going to blackmail us?

ANTHONY: I can stop this—

There's this one girl—she's disappeared—no family—long history of abuse—

I just need to falsify a couple of documents—Then the department will confirm that she's real—but they can't say who it actually is—that'd go against all sorts of privacy laws—but they'll confirm that she exists.

Beat.

MIRI: What are your demands?

ANTHONY: I want her back.

I wanna go where she goes. I wanna nurture her. I wanna take care of her. I wanna have a say in how she feels.

I want to go on the tours—I want an apology—

I just want her to love me.

MIRI: It's rank.

ANTHONY: Alright then. I want to be Currah's husband!

Beat.

You might hate me but Currah will love me.

Beat.

MIRI: Fine. Fine. Let's do it. I don't care—I'll marry you—just don't let's stop.

I *love* this—this is the best thing that's ever happened to me. *I am this!* All those bastards out there—they wouldn't have spat on me—and now they fucken love it!

Fine—I'll marry you—I'll talk about you every day—but let's keep doing it.

Beat.

RONNIE: So Currah discovers the social worker's the man. The department validates her existence. It's not enough—

MIRI: What do you mean?

RONNIE: The problem with setting up a confessional brand is you gotta keep confessing. The 'I loved being raped' shtick—it's tired. They're going to move onto something new…

Beat.

MIRI: We'll find something else—we just need to think of it—

ANTHONY: Currah can marry me.

Realise that I'm a good man after all.

MIRI: Maybe, yes. She learns to understand what the love of a good man can do—

ANTHONY: That love helps her understand the enormity of her previous mistakes.

MIRI: Yes. She's been trash too long and it's time to pull herself out of that gutter—and—and—and I think that Currah needs to heal.

RONNIE: Yes—I can see that.

Realise that she has—Abuse Addiction.

MIRI: Yes, Abuse Addiction.

ANTHONY: Her loving man could help her realise she has Abuse Addiction.

RONNIE: And as luck would have it—her loving man is the man she thought she hated all along—

MIRI: She pushed him away initially because she hated herself—

RONNIE: Yes, she hated herself.

ANTHONY: And he forgives her hateful lies because she hates herself—but he loves her despite all that. And now he can help her to love herself as well as him.

MIRI: And help her heal from her—bipolar!

RONNIE: Yes, her bipolar.

She talks a lot about her bipolar and her shame and her need to heal from her horrific Abuse Addiction.

MIRI: And she realises she needs to connect with her family!

ANTHONY: Her man helps her see she needs to connect with her family!

RONNIE: Yes—there's nothing better than having a man to love and going and reconciling with your family.

MIRI: Your long-lost Indigenous family!

ANTHONY: I make you see your family because I love you and care for you and want you to be the best you can be.

MIRI: My man makes me see my long-lost family and I realise I am someone to love.

Beat.

RONNIE: Your mother—how sick is she?

ANTHONY: She's sick.

MIRI: Yes, my mother can do it—

ANTHONY: What are you talking about?

MIRI: My mother could play Currah's long-lost relative.

ANTHONY: Your mother?

MIRI: Yes—my mother!

ANTHONY: She's a sick lady.

MIRI: Don't think you understand my family because you visited for half an hour once a month.

ANTHONY: It's more than you've been visiting!

RONNIE: Bah. It's too dangerous. The more people that know—the more risk.

ANTHONY: We couldn't co-opt anyone else in anyway—

MIRI: She can do it—I know she can—

RONNIE: But can she—how sick is she?

MIRI: She's fine—

ANTHONY: [*simultaneous*] She's really sick.

MIRI: [*simultaneous*] She'll be fine.

ANTHONY: She's on a respirator a lot of the time.

MIRI: She just overdoes it. She'll manage.

I'll talk to her—we'll get her all briefed up—

ANTHONY: Look at you using your own sick mother.

MIRI: I'll say it again—don't think you know anything about me—you've got no right to judge—

ANTHONY: I'll judge if you're behaving like a monster!

MIRI: I AM NOT A MONSTER!

RONNIE: SHUT UP, THE BOTH OF YOU!

> RONNIE *starts laughing.*

Shit Mama.

Oh, boy—Shit Mama.

MIRI: You're not a Shit Mama.

> *Beat.*

RONNIE: See—the thing is—I'm not interested in losers—

Never have been. 'Cause I've never been a loser. Never.

I always won—didn't matter if my father left me out of the will—or my husband fucked my best friend—or he lost all our money to—emus.

(Never ever invest in—emus.)

I haven't stayed in this industry for forty years peddling shit no-one wants to buy.

Winning—it's like an attitude—it attracts itself—winners attract winners.

But Currah—my Lord—she knew how to win while losing. Now that's *special!*

I can't afford for this to come out—I'd be the laughing stock—Regardless, we'll roll the dice.

There's a deadline—an overdue deadline for the memoir sequel—and someone needs to deliver something more shocking, more interesting, more *titillating*, and more—Currah—than we've seen before.

So while we're on the rest of this ridiculous tour, Anthony, you can put out some fires, hire a celebrant and busy yourself writing a sequel—And it's going to be called *Somebody to Love*—and Currah needs to remember long-lost details from her childhood too horrific to have emerged earlier—

Yes. Her father is sure to have had mates, isn't he?

Men like that always have mates—and you know what mates do when mates get together…

More rape—more pain—et cetera et cetera—of course it leads to Abuse Addiction. And the only way to heal is to Come Home. And so by the end of the book Currah will have found a kindly aunt or cousin or Happy Fucking Squirrel who can see that beautiful light shining deep inside Currah

And that Happy Fucking Squirrel will be black and will teach her about her happy spiritual long-lost family roots.

And lo and behold Currah realises she is 'Somebody to Love' and we're going to sell hundreds of thousands if not millions of copies.

And that is the power of acknowledging you're an addict, finding love and Coming Home to your long-lost family!

And neither of you better breathe a goddamned word of this or I swear to God I'll come down so hard it'll make Katrina look like overcast and cloudy with light showers.

Have I made myself clear?

    Beat.

Good God—no wonder people commit abuse.

And now I've got one more question—one more question and then I'll shut the fuck up.

Champagne?

SCENE FOUR POINT ONE

One year later.

TYRELLE *does a video for YouTube.*

TYRELLE: Assholes!

There are so many assholes, right. That bitch that fired me—asshole—she said—you can work here but can you tone down the camp black gay thing. Honey—that's what I am—a stupid fucking camp black queenie faggot.

That's what I'd say to myself in rehab. Stupid fucking camp black queenie faggot! Own it. Love it. I'd say—please don't call me Tyrelle. Call me a stupid fucking camp black queenie faggot. Own it. Love it. And I'd read Currah's book. Back-to-back. It—helped me. I knew her, you know? I remember when her story first came across my desk! If you haven't read her new book, *Somebody to Love*, go out and get yourself a copy immediately. Abuse Addiction. God, it sure beats being a boring ole crack whore like me, right—

Quote. 'Five men in a room. A sawn-off shotgun. And a girl on her knees. Of course they put it in my mouth. It was time to show 'em how good I was. But I couldn't please them—never please them enough—and so they got real mad. And that's when they smashed the stock of the shotgun in my face.' End Quote.

I learned it. I couldn't help it. It's not like I've been packraped or nothing—well never with a shotgun—but—I guess it's the same thing that got me here too, in a way—I'd been hitting the pipe a bit hard, you know—so I could—lose myself—and it's funny how far you can let yourself—fall—

Quote. 'Please. Please let me find *Somebody to Love*.' End quote.

Currah is the sweetest person I've ever met. She's sweet and funny and real. Get this—I called her up—told her people what had happened—she's so busy doing publicity and all she didn't have time for an interview—but her representatives said I can go meet with her new-found Indigenous family! Isn't that amazing. I get to meet Currah's family! Y'all gonna need to check it out!

Anyways—I should go climb twelve steps or something. Peace.

♦ ♦ ♦ ♦ ♦

A five-star hotel suite. By far the most opulent of all the previous scenes.
CURRAH *has made it.*

It is late at night. MIRI *is in a long, white, luxury dressing-gown. It should look slightly ludicrous… She is on the hotel phone talking to her mother.*

MIRI: [*on the phone*] And how was it—did you like being on camera? That was fun—right?

I know you've had to do a lot of interviews but this one was for a—

Tyrelle—yeah, the black fella—he was nice to you, right?

He's a good guy, Mum—I told you that—and you got to be on TV again!

Well—on YouTube—it's similar.

What do you want me to do, Mum?

I said I'd get you back, I got you back—you're with Aunty Neane and the uncles now—

You know what's she's like—course she's being mean to you.

You're keeping her mouth shut, aren't you?—remember who's paying for all this hey.

Don't cry, Mum—please—I haven't gone anywhere—I'm just—away—

I told you—I'm busy—

> *A knock at the door.*

Mum—I gotta go—okay—I gotta go—

No—you can't call me—

I'll call you in a bit—yeah.

You too.

> *She hangs up the phone.*

> *She moves to the door.* ANTHONY *is standing there.*

ANTHONY: I'm—sorry—I lost track of—

MIRI: Where were you—?

ANTHONY: You just want me to stand here?

MIRI: You reek of booze—

ANTHONY: I want a drink—

MIRI: I'll order you room service—you need to eat something—

ANTHONY: Can we please just get this over with?

> *Beat.*

> MIRI *moves to a hotel drawer—pulls out some documents.*

So what are they this time?

MIRI: Same old—look through 'em if you want.

> *She sits at the table. Collects her fountain pen.*

ANTHONY: Does the *New Yorker* want you to become a columnist?

> MIRI *is silent.*

I can't wait to try out one of Currah's recipes—Currah's Curry?

MIRI: You're being silly.

ANTHONY: Maybe you should release a set of steak knives?

You can case them in my back.

MIRI: You just need to sign here, here and here—

ANTHONY: Where it says 'sign here'.

MIRI: That's right.

And initial every page.

> ANTHONY *cries.*

What do you want me to say?—I'm sorry, Ant—we did the wedding—we released the photos and traffic fell by three per cent on Currah dot com.

ANTHONY: It's only three per cent—

MIRI: So I discovered I could write her myself—It's a good thing, Ant—think of all the time you'll have on your hands now that I can handle all this business—it's a really great opportunity for you—

ANTHONY: Look at you.

MIRI: What?

ANTHONY: You're so pretty.

MIRI: Stop it, Ant—

ANTHONY: My name's Anthony—

I'm so stupid.

MIRI: You're not stupid.

ANTHONY: And which one is that? Miri or *Currah?*

> *Beat.*

CURRAH: What's the difference?

> *Beat.*

ANTHONY: I'm so stupid—I don't know why I never got this. Some people only ever get to look in at the window.

> *Beat.*

MIRI: How 'bout we get you some help—?

I'll pay.

ANTHONY: I can't do this anymore.

MIRI: I know.

ANTHONY: I'm nothing.

MIRI: We'll only need your signature a couple more times and then you'll be done. Take a holiday.

> *Beat.*

ANTHONY: It was meant to be beautiful.

MIRI: And it is beautiful.

Thank you, Ant. Thank you.

> *Beat.*

ANTHONY: I don't know why I love you.

> *He signs.*

All done.

The autograph can leave the building…

MIRI: Thank you, Ant—

Take care of yourself—

> ANTHONY *has left.*
>
> *She picks up the phone.*

[*On the phone*] Shit, Ronnie—he was filthy drunk again—

> *She laughs.*

That's exactly what he's like!

SCENE FOUR POINT TWO

The next morning. Same room.

TYRELLE *and* RONNIE. TYRELLE *is setting up his camera on a tripod.*

RONNIE: You look tired.

TYRELLE: I am tired.

RONNIE: Burning the candle?

TYRELLE: You know how things get—

RONNIE: You shouldn't work yourself so hard.

> *Beat.*

She'll be out in a moment—

TYRELLE: I'm in no hurry.

No hurry at all…

> CURRAH *enters—cool, aloof, sophisticated, a woman now in full control of her powers. She's by far the most glamorous we've seen her.*

CURRAH: Hello, Tyrelle.

TYRELLE: Oh. My. God.

RONNIE: You look amazing.

TYRELLE: You really do.

Amazing.

RONNIE: Beautiful.

TYRELLE: What happened to sordid heroin chic goes walkabout?

RONNIE: Yes—what did happen to her?

CURRAH: She grew up.

> *Beat.*

Leave us awhile.

RONNIE: I'd prefer to stay—

CURRAH: It's so good to see you, Tyrelle.

> *She gives him an efficiently warm kiss.*

It was awful hearing about your—you know—

TYRELLE: I know.

CURRAH: I'm so glad we can do a follow-up—help your—situation.

RONNIE: Next year it'll be world peace!

CURRAH: Did you want a coffee, Tyrelle?

TYRELLE: No—I'm… [fine]

CURRAH: I'll have a latte, Ronnie. Soy. Double strength.

Dash of caramel.

[*To* TYRELLE] You sure, Ronnie's going?

RONNIE: Am I?

CURRAH: What do you want, Tyrelle?

RONNIE: I could call room service?

CURRAH: I need a real coffee, Ronnie, not the cats' piss they serve here.

[*To* TYRELLE] What are you having?

TYRELLE: I'm fine.

CURRAH: No really—what do you want?

RONNIE: I'm going anyway apparently.

CURRAH: I'll have some cakey things too.

I feel like cakey things.

TYRELLE: No really, I'm fine.

CURRAH: He'll have the same as me.

Thanks, Ronnie, you're a legend.

RONNIE: I'll leave you to it.

CURRAH: [*to* TYRELLE] You're really going to love it.

RONNIE *leaves.*

Beat.

She's a dear.

When Ronnie told me about all this I was so happy to help. I mean you practically discovered me—so I'm really glad we can do this—properly this time—

TYRELLE: Camera and everything.

CURRAH: Gosh, we've come a long way, haven't we…?

TYRELLE: You certainly have.

CURRAH: And you—don't forget you—

TYRELLE: Not really.

CURRAH: But you have. I know that in my heart.

It's such a journey, isn't it? Life.

TYRELLE *turns on the camera.*

TYRELLE: I remember when I first met you four years ago. You were a very different girl then—shy, stammering, nervous.

CURRAH: Oh God—I'd rather forget that!

TYRELLE: And now some people are claiming you're an egotistical megalomaniac who viciously protects her own image. What do you say to that?

> *Beat.*

CURRAH: Um—I don't think that's—

TYRELLE: Because you do—don't you—protect your image?

CURRAH: What's going on here—?

TYRELLE: I don't know, honey—I guess what I want is—well—

I want to unearth the *real* Currah—the one the public doesn't get to see.

> *Beat.*

CURRAH: I think my success—is because I am who I am—

TYRELLE: And you've just released your second memoir?

CURRAH: Yes—

TYRELLE: *Somebody to Love*

CURRAH: That's right. *Somebody to Love.*

TYRELLE: So tell me, sweetheart—who is this Somebody—

CURRAH: I know it's hard to believe, but it's me!

TYRELLE: How personal!

CURRAH: Oh, it was—

Someone—with my—background—I don't mind saying this—it can be hard to love yourself—this book chronicles my journey away from Abuse Addiction to finding true Self Love.

TYRELLE: [*acid Whitney Houston*] 'It is the greatest love of all'—

So how did you learn to love yourself?

CURRAH: Well—I—I—

TYRELLE: Fess up.

CURRAH: I was encouraged to find my family—

TYRELLE: Your long-lost Indigenous family!

CURRAH: Who you just had the privilege of meeting—

TYRELLE: It was a highlight of my year!

CURRAH: Connecting with them again was like—Coming Home.

TYRELLE: Oh, I can understand why—

CURRAH: And you met my Aunty Wanda?

TYRELLE: What an amazing woman!

CURRAH: She is right. And Aunty Neaney and the uncles…

TYRELLE: So down-to-earth.

CURRAH: I guess that's where I get it from!

TYRELLE: It was so great—we were having a beer and your mom—

CURRAH: You mean my aunty—Aunty Wanda.

TYRELLE: Oh yes. That's right. Silly me.

CURRAH: Aunty Wanda and Aunty Neaney.

TYRELLE: You're right.

I just don't understand why they kept on referring to you as Miri?

Beat.

CURRAH: That was my mum's nickname before she was taken—

TYRELLE: That's getting a bit far-fetched, isn't it?

CURRAH: You know what they say.

Truth is stranger than fiction…

TYRELLE: Oh, I just want the truth.

CURRAH: And you have it—

TYRELLE: Please just let me see the real Currah.

CURRAH: She's right in front of you…

TYRELLE: [*whispering*] Just admit it to me—baby—

Just tell me—

CURRAH: There's nothing to tell—

TYRELLE: [*whispering*] I just wanna understand why—

CURRAH: There's nothing to understand—

TYRELLE: [*whispering*] Let me in on the secret—

CURRAH: There is no secret.

TYRELLE: [*whispering*] You can just include me in the joke—

CURRAH: There's no joke here.

TYRELLE: You won't even tell me why?

CURRAH: I don't know what you're talking about?

TYRELLE: I thought you would—I knew you would—I—

CURRAH: I'm lost—

TYRELLE: I can't believe you won't include me—after everything I've done for you...

> *Beat.*

CURRAH: You know, sometimes there's like—well—metaphorical truth.

TYRELLE: Metaphorical truth?

CURRAH: Sometimes something is deeply true, even if it's not one hundred per cent solely accurate.

TYRELLE: Then it's not true.

CURRAH: Well, it should be.

See, if you look at things too closely you can make them dirty.

TYRELLE: Dirty?

CURRAH: Please, Tyrelle—don't make things dirty.

> *Beat.*

TYRELLE: You're real name is Miri Smith and you were hired by Anthony Dooley to play the role of Currah, who was in actual fact created and written by Anthony. You were never abused as a child.

> *Beat.*

CURRAH: That's ludicrous—

TYRELLE: Just because I love you doesn't mean I'm not a journalist, dear—

CURRAH: Where's Ronnie gone with our coffee?

TYRELLE: Believe me—I don't want to do this—

CURRAH: Then don't.

TYRELLE: But now I feel—if I don't—break this story—

CURRAH: You don't have to—

TYRELLE: Then thousands of kids are going to think anything's possible— and we both know that it's not.

> *Beat.*

CURRAH: If you work hard enough / then—

> TYRELLE *laughs.*

TYRELLE: Oh yes—I've heard that one my whole life—you can do anything—you just gotta work hard...

CURRAH: My story is an inspiration to thousands—

TYRELLE: An inspiration for who? For you?

CURRAH: Lots of people want to trade in gossip and lies and they can believe what they like. But the real question everyone should ask is—do you want to believe in my story?

> *Beat.*

TYRELLE: It would be nice—to believe—in something—

CURRAH: Yes.

TYRELLE: It would be nice to know that something—couldn't be taken away from you—for once—

CURRAH: Well, I'm here, Tyrelle, and I'm not going anywhere and you can always rely on me! Because I'm real—you make me real—

TYRELLE: BUT YOU'RE NOT YOU!

CURRAH: I AM I AM I AM.

TYRELLE: You're NOT!

CURRAH: I AM!

TYRELLE: You're Miri Smith!

CURRAH: I'm not her—

TYRELLE: That's who you are!

CURRAH: I'm not her—

TYRELLE: That's you!

CURRAH: I'll never be her.

TYRELLE: What's wrong with Miri Smith?

CURRAH: You haven't got *time* to hear about—her.

TYRELLE: Try me—

CURRAH: You'd need so much *time*.

TYRELLE: I've got time—

CURRAH: She's shit—she's—she's—poor and she's depressed and she doesn't know anyone and she doesn't have friends and she doesn't go out and she doesn't have a dad and she's—shy—and—and—she *hates* her mother.

TYRELLE: That's not such a bad thing.

CURRAH: She hates her mother!

TYRELLE: I hate my mother!

CURRAH: And she hates everything.

TYRELLE: I hate everything.

CURRAH: And it doesn't matter anyway.
BECAUSE MY NAME IS CURRAH!

Beat.

TYRELLE: Oh, my God.

CURRAH: What?

TYRELLE: That's sad—that's so sad—I didn't think—

CURRAH: Tyrelle—

TYRELLE *holds up a kitbag.*

TYRELLE: Look familiar?

CURRAH *doesn't answer.*

LOOK FAMILIAR?

CURRAH: I—yes—

TYRELLE: The famous Adidas kitbag.

CURRAH: Yes—that's right—

TYRELLE: The one your daddy used.

CURRAH: With his mates—

TYRELLE: And you know what else right—

TYRELLE *starts to laugh nervously—before leaning back and shutting his eyes—*

CURRAH: What? What is it?

TYRELLE: I don't know if I can do this.

CURRAH: Do what?

TYRELLE: I'm scared.

CURRAH: What are you scared of?

TYRELLE: FUCK!
Do you remember this?

He reaches inside the bag and pulls out a sawn-off shotgun.

He aims it at MIRI's *head.*

MIRI: What are you doing?

TYRELLE: I don't know.

MIRI: Why do you have a gun?

TYRELLE: Why do you think?

MIRI: I don't know why you've got a fucking gun.

TYRELLE: And I don't know why you lied!

MIRI: I didn't lie…

TYRELLE: Does this bring back the memories?

MIRI: Yes—I don't—

TYRELLE: 'Cause you never experienced it?

MIRI: I don't know—

TYRELLE: A sawn-off shotgun—
That your father made you fellate—

MIRI: That my father made me fellate—

TYRELLE: Before he pack-raped you—

MIRI: Before he pack-raped me—
Yes.

> *Beat.*

> RONNIE *enters the room holding a tray of coffee.*

RONNIE: I bought chocolate mud cake—

> *Beat.*

> [*Uncertain*] You've don't like mud cake?

MIRI: Do what he says, Ronnie.

RONNIE: [*to* TYRELLE] Why are you holding a gun?

TYRELLE: Put the coffee down.

RONNIE: What's going on?

TYRELLE: SHUT THE FUCK UP, RONNIE.

CURRAH: Just do what he says.

TYRELLE: CURRAH'S TAKING A TRIP DOWN MEMORY LANE!

> TYRELLE *turns on the TV and shows his previously shot footage of* MIRI*'s sick mother.*

MIRI'S MUM: [*voice-over*] She's a good girl, my girl—

TYRELLE: [*voice-over*] Who is?

MIRI'S MUM: [*voice-over*] Miri looks after her mum.

TYRELLE: [*voice-over*] And who's Miri?

MIRI'S MUM: [*voice-over*] You know—that girl—what is it I'm supposed to call her—?

I can't remember.

      MIRI'S MUM *bursts into a spasm of coughing.*

TYRELLE: [*voice-over*] You're supposed to call her something?

MIRI'S MUM: [*voice-over*] Currah—that's right—that's her name—

Don't tell Miri I said that—

TYRELLE: [*voice-over*] I won't say a word—

MIRI'S MUM: [*voice-over*] Oh, good—she'd be so mad at me—

TYRELLE: [*voice-over*] Why would she be mad?

CURRAH: So she sometimes calls me Miri—

TYRELLE: Is it your mum?

CURRAH: It's my Aunty Wanda.

TYRELLE: It's your mum—

CURRAH: MY MUM'S DEAD—

TYRELLE: She's right there—

CURRAH: SHE'S DEAD!

TYRELLE: She's just a sick, old woman.

CURRAH: Do you really think I'd have someone like that for a mum?!

     Beat.

TYRELLE: Are you a racist?

CURRAH: No!

TYRELLE: Is this some self-loathing race thing?

CURRAH: No!

     Beat.

TYRELLE: So what then?—I'm trying to understand—Are you a psychopath?

CURRAH: No.

TYRELLE: Was it just for shits and giggles?

CURRAH: No.

TYRELLE: Were you LAUGHING at us the whole time?

CURRAH: I'm not laughing—and I'm not going to explain myself—

TYRELLE: But you have to—I'm one of the people that buys your books!

> *Beat.*

Get on your knees—

CURRAH: What?

TYRELLE: On your knees!

CURRAH: What are you—?

What—?

RONNIE: Tyrelle—

TYRELLE: I'm just gonna help you understand—

CURRAH: Understand what?

TYRELLE: What it feels like to be abused—

Now blow it!

MIRI: What?

TYRELLE: BLOW MY FUCKING GUN, BITCH!

> MIRI, *degraded, on her knees, tentatively puts her lips near the edge of the shotgun.*

Are you excited?

MIRI: No.

TYRELLE: Do you want to give yourself to me?

MIRI: No.

TYRELLE: Would that make you enjoy it?

MIRI: No.

TYRELLE: Come on—put your lips around it!

> MIRI *puts her lips around the shotgun—she's crying.*

Now suck it. Deep.

Now look up at me. And say, 'Daddy, I love you'.

Say it. With me down your throat.

MIRI: [*chokingly*] Daddy, I love you.

TYRELLE: I love you too, baby girl.

I DIDN'T TELL YOU YOU COULD STOP!

You liking it, Ronnie?

RONNIE: You know I don't—

TYRELLE: You enjoy it?

RONNIE: No, Tyrelle—

> TYRELLE *pushes* MIRI *off the gun.*

TYRELLE: Because this is what this smut *actually* looks like—

RONNIE: Yes, Tyrelle—

TYRELLE: And it's not as pretty now is it—?

RONNIE: It's just business—the market wants it—you give 'em what they want—

You know—business, Tyrelle.

TYRELLE: I know business, Ronnie.

> *He picks up the gun and is about to smash it into* MIRI*'s face.*
>
> *She screams and he lowers the gun.*

That's the business we're in.

RONNIE: Currah's not about this—she's about redemption—

TYRELLE: You've made yourself a rich woman from these people!

RONNIE: People need to believe in redemption!

TYRELLE: You revitalised your *career* on—on a—hoax?

RONNIE: I can't help it if so many people want it dirty—

I don't choose what sells. If they wanna pay for it—

Why shouldn't we give them a thrill?!

> TYRELLE *moves swiftly across the room and smacks the stock of his gun hard into* MIRI*'s jaw—*
>
> *It makes a sickening thud.*
>
> MIRI *wails.*

TYRELLE: Is that thrilling?

RONNIE: For God's sake—

TYRELLE: Was that thrilling to you?

RONNIE: No.

TYRELLE: 'Cause really—it's cold and scary and lonely and—mediocre.

RONNIE: Yes.

TYRELLE: And that might seem profound in the privacy of your own home—but in the real world it's just brutal and dull.

RONNIE: Yes—

TYRELLE: But fantasising about it whilst reading on the couch—feeling superior because it's not you—that's another form of abuse—

RONNIE: Yes.

TYRELLE: Enjoying our misery—

Those of us who struggle—who have more to fight for—

More prejudice—more mental illness—more pain—

And our suffering is there for your enjoyment.

RONNIE: Surely we need to—comprehend—what people go through—

TYRELLE: This is what people go through—

He advances towards RONNIE.

She screams and backs away, falling behind the bed.

RONNIE: Please, Tyrelle—I'm an old woman—

TYRELLE: You can still learn—

RONNIE: Don't let him kill me!

MIRI: Tyrelle—

TYRELLE *kicks her violently three times in the chest and stomach.*

RONNIE *is wailing.*

TYRELLE: THIS IS WHAT IT'S LIKE!

MIRI: Tyrelle!

TYRELLE: WHAT?!

MIRI: I know this isn't you—

TYRELLE: What?

MIRI: I know—we've—we've pushed a button—I know we've upset you—but I know you're not like this—

TYRELLE: What am I like?

MIRI: You're sweet and loving and caring and funny and—and—

TYRELLE: And what?

MIRI: And I think you've had a hard time—

TYRELLE: Really?

MIRI: I think you've done it really tough—I think you've paid a big price—

Beat.

TYRELLE: Do you think I'm doing this because I was abused?

Beat.

MIRI: Maybe?

TYRELLE: Do you think that maybe I read your book—every fucking day—in rehab.

MIRI: You could have—

TYRELLE: And that I'd cry while I read it and think—'shit—if she can, then so can I'!

MIRI: Were you—were you, Tyrelle?

Abused as a child?

Beat.

TYRELLE: WOULDN'T YOU LIKE TO KNOW?!

Beat.

MIRI: What do you want, Tyrelle?

TYRELLE: I want to have the chances you've got—

MIRI: Maybe Currah was the exception. Maybe she was the one that got to do it for us.

RONNIE *struggles to pull herself up onto the bed—she's hurt and shaken.*

RONNIE: I don't know what happened—

A pool of piss is leaking out from behind the bed.

TYRELLE: What have you *done?*

RONNIE: I don't know what—

It just happened—

TYRELLE: You pissed your pants?

You pissed your fucking pants?

RONNIE: I'm so—I don't know what—

MIRI: What do you want?

Please tell us what you want?

Beat.

TYRELLE: I want you to say it—on camera—

I want you to admit that Currah is nobody—

MIRI: I'm not strong enough to kill her—what would I have then?

RONNIE: For God's sake, just do it.

Beat.

CURRAH: I can't—

TYRELLE: See—right at this minute—in this room—we've got a few things that can make us achieve something really powerful.

A camera. And a gun.

And we can do something rare, something memorable—and who cares if we're the only ones that see it—?

Let's shoot something—real—without spin—for old time's sake—Either way, you're going to get shot.

Silence.

MIRI *stares at the camera but cannot speak.*

TYRELLE *is off somewhere—wryly and sadly amused.*

And you never know—maybe it'll take off and I'll become really famous?

RONNIE: Maybe—

TYRELLE: Maybe I'll be just like Currah?!

[*Heartbroken*] And wouldn't that be a laugh.

Beat.

And that's your cue.

Beat.

MIRI: [*huge, racking, heaving sobs*] I don't like where I'm from—I don't like what I am—I just wanted to be somebody else—and I'm—so sorry...

SCENE FIVE

Six months later.

ANTHONY *reads a letter to the editor written by* MIRI.

Perhaps MIRI *is still on stage...*

ANTHONY: [*reading*] 'A lot has been said since my video with Tyrelle went viral a few months ago...

Yeah, I did turn down a job at *Harper's Bazaar*. No I'm not private school-educated. And yes I am speaking with my mum.

I know there's been a lot of criticism of Anthony Dooley and Ronnie Lowe. All I can say is let's not judge them too harshly—they can't help being who they are. Let's feel sorry for them, instead of crucifying them. It's the right thing to do.

See, in many ways, aren't we all trying to be something we're not? Aren't we all, in our own ways, trying to be more than what we are? To my fans—and the peeps that love me—

Don't worry about me, although I know you will. A great opportunity has just opened up and I really think it's going to be the best thing I've ever done. I can't tell you any more at this stage but it's in America and you're going to DIE when you see it.

To my haters—and my Anthony, I say—

You may think you know what it's like to be me and why I did what I did—but you'll never really know.

The way it feels inside my skin can only ever be known to me.

And I'm not going to explain—or apologise—or clarify what I've done to anyone, least of all you.

I'm complicated.

I'm Nobody's Girl.'

    Beat.

    ANTHONY *rips up the paper viciously.*

♦ ♦ ♦ ♦ ♦

A dilapidated hotel room, very inferior to the glorious hotel rooms of the previous scenes.

The paper and debris strewn from TYRELLE'*s tirade in the previous scene remain.*

A computer also lies destroyed on the ground.

ANTHONY *sits, looking at the mess.*

RONNIE: Ant? Please—open the door—

    ANTHONY *opens the door.*

Hello.

ANTHONY: Hi.

RONNIE: Do you mind if I come in?

ANTHONY: Suit yourself.

> RONNIE *walks into the room.*

RONNIE: [*dryly*] Moved up in the world?

ANTHONY: I never got around to cleaning up—

RONNIE: Did they find what they were looking for?

ANTHONY: They must have. I'm being sued.

RONNIE: I heard. Fraud.

You'll be fine.

ANTHONY: We'll see.

RONNIE: You never returned my phone calls—

ANTHONY: Well, there wasn't much point was there—?

> *Beat.*

RONNIE: I haven't been back that long—only a couple of weeks—

ANTHONY: You certainly went very quiet while all the media stuff was going down—

RONNIE: I wasn't in the country. I was on a—leave of absence.

Personal circumstances.

ANTHONY: I heard rumours?

RONNIE: Oh?

ANTHONY: Tyrelle—

Your nervous breakdown—

> *Beat.*

RONNIE: Oh. That.

Yes—well—I guess we all have our challenges.

Three months in the Maldives waiting for it to all blow over.

ANTHONY: It's not blowing over.

RONNIE: I know it's not.

> *Beat.*

ANTHONY: Did you—*want* something?

RONNIE: Yes—right—look, Ant—

ANTHONY: Anthony.

RONNIE: Ant—I had a revelation—in the Maldives—you'll like this—

After three months I was so bored I craved a hold-up with a sawn-off shotgun! Well, no not really.

Anyway—after a lot of navel-gazing, I realised—we've got to keep on living, don't we? No matter how much we think we've fucked it up or life has fucked us up—we've just got to keep on doing it. Living. Fighting. Life is like an addiction.

ANTHONY: I guess.

RONNIE: How is the writing going?

ANTHONY: You've got to be kidding?

RONNIE: You must keep writing!

ANTHONY: I'm no more a writer than you're a—good agent.

RONNIE: I'm really sorry to hear that—I think you're—highly talented.

    Beat.

I bought you a present—

    She gives him a bottle of champagne.

ANTHONY: I don't much go in for champagne anymore—

RONNIE: Ah—one never goes in for champagne—one just gets used to drinking it.

The secret is just open your gullet and let it pour right down your throat.

No need to even taste it.

    Beat.

You'll never get her back.

    Beat.

ANTHONY: For a day—just one day—I thought they were going to side with me.

RONNIE: That girl has charisma.

ANTHONY: I think she still believes I ratted her out—but I didn't—

RONNIE: I know you didn't. I did.

What's better than a great hoax, I thought?

A great hoax revelation!

Tyrelle played me the tape. I gave him the interview.

Think of the units we'd have sold. The publicity.

That was the thinking at least.

Who knew he'd—take it so personally?

ANTHONY: Well, it's set him up—

RONNIE: Yes—it has.

> *Beat.*

I did some research—

I didn't know both your parents were dead—

ANTHONY: Yes—

RONNIE: That must be very sad for you—

ANTHONY: I guess.

RONNIE: Pretty much alone—

So no-one can contradict your story…

ANTHONY: Not that it matters—

RONNIE: These things always matter. You spoke a truth with Currah. And it worked.

But people need to understand why.

> *Beat.*

ANTHONY: Do you know Currer Bell?

RONNIE: Who?

ANTHONY: Currer Bell.

RONNIE: Who's Currer Bell?

ANTHONY: History's forgotten him but he was huge at the time. No-one would touch Charlotte Bronte. She was a woman. So she was ignored. But she was brilliant, so she did what she had to do. She created a male to write *Jane Eyre*. His name was Currer Bell. Currer Bell wrote *Jane Eyre*.

And that's why I named her Currah.

Those bastards out there win. I'm done. I'm a racist, predator fuck.

> *Beat.*

RONNIE: When I was young—my daddy had a party trick. We had a pool—it was the envy of the neighbourhood. Often we had barbeques surrounding the pool—

ANTHONY: What does this have to do…?

RONNIE: Hold on! This is important…

But he wasn't a happy man. Oh no. He didn't like me much—I was strong-willed.

So he'd make a show of it.

With everyone around—he'd sneak up on me, grab me by the scruff of the neck and hurtle me down to the bottom.

I'd be beating his chest, beating at him while he held me on the bottom of the pool.

I thought I was going to drown, I'd breathe in the water—

And eventually he'd release me and I'd run out of the pool, terrorised, and everyone would start to laugh.

I felt like nothing.

> *Beat.*

You should remember that. Remember it.

It's stories like that that make us connect to your work.

> *Beat.*

ANTHONY: Did that really happen?

RONNIE: What does it matter?

> *Beat.*

People just want to know—why the people do the bad things.

> *A knock on the door.*

Someone needs to see you.

ANTHONY: Miri?

RONNIE: Our names are mud. We've got to stop with this—*pretence*—it's time for the truth.

The truth always heals.

> *She opens the door, revealing* TYRELLE—*who looks the most elegant and stylish we've seen him—clearly he's found success—and he wears it like he never knew anything else.*

> RONNIE *involuntarily recoils—it is the first time she's seen him since the incident.*

TYRELLE: I was so glad to get your message—it has been too long.

RONNIE: [*steadily*] You remember Ant, don't you?

TYRELLE: How could I forget? The Great White Hoaxer. Anthony.

RONNIE: Oh no, you're mistaken. It's Ant.

TYRELLE: Ant?

RONNIE: Everyone calls him Ant.

TYRELLE: Ant?

ANTHONY: Yes, Ant.

TYRELLE: Okay then—Ant.

> *Beat.*

> RONNIE *tries to speak—but cannot.*

> *Clearly having* TYRELLE *in the room is a problem for her.*

How are you?

RONNIE: One second—

TYRELLE: I thought you were going to like hate me forever or something.

RONNIE: Oh God, this is hard—

TYRELLE: Come and give me a hug!

RONNIE: (Don't fucking touch me!)

> *Beat.*

> RONNIE, *with great effort, squashes her panic and continues.*

No. It's nothing.

TYRELLE: Why did you want to see me, Ronnie?

RONNIE: Ant has something to tell you, Tyrelle—something important.

TYRELLE: I really do only have a minute—I've got to get back to the studio—

RONNIE: This really does explain everything.

TYRELLE: I normally have an assistant do this now, but okay—

Let's hear what you've got...

ANTHONY: Ronnie?

RONNIE: Just think of what they're saying about us—about you!

TYRELLE. I don't know if I'll have any space on the show but we'll see.

You wanted to tell me something, Ant?

ANTHONY: I don't know.

RONNIE: Don't be scared—don't be afraid of the truth—

Tell him why you did what you did.

Why you created Currah

ANTHONY: Why?

RONNIE: Tell him what you told me—

Tell him about your father—

TYRELLE: Your father?

ANTHONY: My father.

RONNIE: And the pool.

The pool, Ant, tell Tyrelle about your father and the pool.

Beat.

ANTHONY: I can't.

RONNIE: You can, Ant. Just tell the truth.

TYRELLE: You can tell me.

Help me understand.

ANTHONY: I—I—

When I was young my father used to hold parties.

RONNIE: Parties!

ANTHONY: And there would be the pool.

TYRELLE: The pool.

ANTHONY: And my—my father—

RONNIE: Your father—

ANTHONY: He didn't like me very much—

RONNIE: No, he didn't.

ANTHONY: He didn't like me at all—

RONNIE: Cruel Dad.

Cruel Daddy.

ANTHONY: And he wanted to make me pay.

TYRELLE: You were his little boy.

ANTHONY: His little boy.

And I would be swimming—

RONNIE: So happy—

TYRELLE: So happy—

ANTHONY: Swimming and playing and—

TYRELLE: Laughing—

RONNIE: Laughing and playing like a happy little boy.

ANTHONY: And Dad—

RONNIE: Daddy—

ANTHONY: Daddy hated seeing his son happy.

RONNIE: That's right.

ANTHONY: And he wanted to make his son sad.

RONNIE: So sad.

ANTHONY: And—and—

RONNIE: And what, Ant?

>*Beat.*

ANTHONY: I can't.

RONNIE: You can, Ant.

TYRELLE: You can.

>Help us understand.

>Help me understand.

RONNIE: There's nothing to be afraid of anymore…

>You're amongst—friends.

>*Beat.*

ANTHONY: And while I was playing in the pool—

>With all those people all around—

>Dad—

RONNIE: Daddy—

ANTHONY: Daddy came into the pool—

>And he looked at me like I was nothing—

>And he wanted me to be nothing—

>He wanted me to know I was nothing—

RONNIE: Nothing without him.

ANTHONY: Nothing without him.

>And he swam up to me like a shark—

>A shark circling his prey.

>And while I was playing—

RONNIE: A sweet little boy—

ANTHONY: A sweet little boy playing—

>Daddy came up to me and he grabbed me—

By the neck—

Daddy grabbed me by the neck and down down down we went—

RONNIE: All the way down—

ANTHONY: Right to the bottom of the pool—

And through the water I could hear the people—

They were—

RONNIE: Laughing—

ANTHONY: Yes. Laughing.

And Daddy held me on the bottom of the pool—

And my little arms were beating at his chest—

And I wanted to love him I wanted his love I just wanted his approval but he was so big and powerful—so big and powerful—a big and powerful man leeching the life right from me and forcing the flood into my lungs—

The blue of the water—the bottom of the pool—the stars in my eyes—

I was drifting—and I knew—

I was nothing—

RONNIE: Nobody.

ANTHONY: Nobody.

No-one's.

And all I could hear were the people. Laughing. Hysterically laughing at me.

RONNIE: Laughing at Daddy's little game.

ANTHONY: Laughing at Daddy's little game.

And the nothing son he hated.

Beat.

TYRELLE: So hard.

So harrowing.

ANTHONY: So—

RONNIE: Difficult—yes difficult—

TYRELLE: Distressing—

RONNIE: But you survived—

ANTHONY: Yes—I'm here—

TYRELLE: Yes—you're here—

ANTHONY: I'm here.

TYRELLE: And that's why you created her—

ANTHONY: Yes—

TYRELLE: Because you couldn't cope—

ANTHONY: No—I couldn't cope—

TYRELLE: With your own story.

ANTHONY: My own story—

    Which was so hard.

    So painful.

TYRELLE: So lost.

ANTHONY: Nobody's Boy.

TYRELLE: Nobody's Boy.

RONNIE: Nobody's Boy.

TYRELLE: But now—you're—*stronger*—?

ANTHONY: Yes stronger—

    And now—now—I can.

TYRELLE: You can—?

ANTHONY: I can *share*

TYRELLE: Yes, share!

ANTHONY: Yes, share my story with the world.

TYRELLE: And what a story—

ANTHONY: Share it all with all of you—

TYRELLE: For the good—

ANTHONY: The greater good—

TYRELLE: Yes, the greater good of the world.

ANTHONY: I can share it all with everyone.

TYRELLE: So it never happens again.

RONNIE: So it never happens again.

ANTHONY: So it never happens again.

    Beat.

TYRELLE: It all makes sense now—

RONNIE: Yes—yes—It's good.

    The world will love you.

Finally.
Beat.
Eventually, sadly…
Welcome to the family.

THE END

GRIFFIN THEATRE COMPANY AND
LA BOITE THEATRE COMPANY PRESENT

A HOAX

BY RICK VIEDE

SBW Stables Theatre
20 July – 1 September
A Hoax was first performed at La Boite's
Roundhouse Theatre, Brisbane on 5 May, 2012

Director Lee Lewis
Dramaturg Tahli Corin
Designer Renée Mulder
Design Assistant Melita Lee Yuen
Lighting Designer Jason Glenwright
Music, Sound & AV Designer Steve Toulmin
Fight Choreographer Nigel Poulton

With Charles Allen, Glenn Hazeldine,
Sally McKenzie & Shari Sebbens

I remember sitting in a box office idly surfing the internet. I was cruising for more gossipy details about the bizarre truth of JT LeRoy. I'd heard somewhere of Anthony Godby Johnson and his connection to Armistead Maupin, and the James Frey controversy had played out several years earlier. Jumping through a wiki wormhole I came across the page 'Literary Hoaxes'. Hmm, I thought. My next play.

In my research I identified what I'd call a specific type of hoax. The misery memoir. The fake autobiography. The idealised depiction of difference. These weren't the same as pathological Norma Khouri, historical revisionist Helen Demidenko or prankster Ern Malley; these misery memoir hoaxes played with the very nature of identity. JT, Anthony, Wanda Koolmatrie and Nasdijj were all created by complicated, pained people who felt they lacked access to any form of personal power.

So they took their talent – writing – and created a persona that wielded immense power. These writers have been harshly judged, often publicly reviled, and simplistically explained away as greedy, racist, sexist, delusional and psychotic. Yet their creations show us how fragile the concept of identity is in the modern world and how easily it can be overthrown.

It seems race, sexuality and abuse victim can be nothing more than the creation of a talented writer. Controversial. No wonder they were reviled.

So here is *A Hoax*. It's about four people, four complicated psyches, battling to be seen in the world. These four are desperate for success and acknowledgement and will do anything to get it. They cross races, nationalities, generations, sexualities and genders (one even being beyond gender!). And like all of us, witnessed from afar, their ambitions and scheming are strangely funny.

Restoration comedies sought to uncover the great moral dilemmas of their age. Similarly, *A Hoax* seeks to deconstruct a great dilemma of our age. In a society buzzing with PR noise and where your difference can be exploited to further your personal brand, what lengths would you go to be seen? What would you do to be heard?

Rick Viede

PLAYWRIGHT'S NOTE

One of my favourite plays is a comedy by SN Behrman called *No Time For Comedy*. It was written just before World War II. I found it while I was reading plays from the 1930s looking for evidence of what people in America were thinking about the rise of Nazism.

It's a great story about a famous comedy writer who wants to write a serious play about the politics of the time they are living in but everyone just wants him to keep writing comedy. This piece of writing gives me a window into what a person of that time was thinking. It was a really successful Broadway production so I also know that over 500 people a night sat and watched the ideas of that play. It entertained them, distracted them from the cares of their day, formed part of their conversations for the next week and ultimately helped shape what they thought of their world. This play is a direct connection to the thoughts and the people of that time.

Fifty, sixty, seventy years from now, the new plays that are written and produced will give people then an idea of who we are now. New plays are our treasures which generations to come will inherit. So, people a thousand years from now, in 2011 Rick Viede wrote *A Hoax*. It won the Griffin Award.

I remember when I first read it I was challenged by it, a bit scared by the identity politics he was willing to explore, and convinced that audiences would be similarly engaged. I also laughed, and hoped audiences would too. Then two exceptional Artistic Directors, David Berthold and Sam Strong committed the resources of their two theatre companies, across two states, to put this story in front of audiences in 2012.

Producing new Australian plays at the moment is risky – you never know with a new script whether it will work until you put it onstage – and expensive – and neither company has a lot of money. La Boite and Griffin both have great audiences however, who support new writing and are willing to be challenged and provoked. And if you are reading this play a thousand years from now, know that for six weeks in 2012 in Sydney people were talking about *A Hoax*.

Lee Lewis

DIRECTOR'S NOTE

Rick Viede
Writer and Performer

Rick is an Australian writer and performer. He won the prestigious 2008 Griffin Award for his debut play *Whore*, which premièred in 2009 at Belvoir St Theatre. The Australian production of *Whore* was closely followed by a production at New York's Summer Play Festival at the Public Theatre. In 2010 Rick was awarded the Queensland Premier's Literary Award for *Whore*. For **Griffin Theatre Company:** In 2008, Rick was an Affiliate Playwright with Griffin Theatre Company. At Griffin, he worked on two commissions, *Autumn* and *Poised*, and was commissioned to write a neo-restoration gender-bending comedy for Bell Shakespeare Company. *A Hoax* is Rick's second play, and winner of the 2011 Griffin Award. It was showcased at the National Playwriting Festival in 2011, and receives its official world première in this La Boite and Griffin Theatre Company co-production. **Other Theatre:** Rick also created the satirical 'Aspiring American' character of *Glace Chase* that has played to critical acclaim throughout Australia, including seasons at Belvoir St Downstairs Theatre, Melbourne Comedy Festival, Mardi Gras Festival, The Butterfly Club, and Feast Festival. Glace received a Highly Commended mention at the SPAA Fringe Pitching competition 2010 and was shortlisted for Movie Network's WebFest for Glace Chase VS NY. Rick has also been shortlisted for numerous other awards. **Training:** Rick holds a B.A. from Monash University and a Graduate Diploma in Screenwriting at the Australian Film, Television and Radio School (AFTRS).

Lee Lewis
Director

Theatre: Lee Lewis has recently directed *Twelfth Night* for Bell Shakespeare, *ZEBRA!* and *Honour* for Sydney Theatre Company, *That Face* at Belvoir and *Silent Disco* at Griffin. Other credits include *Love Lies Bleeding* (STC); *Motel* and *Stag* (Wharf2Loud); *The Call* and *The Nightwatchman* (Griffin Theatre Company); *Stoning Mary* (Griffin Independent); *2000 Feet Away, Half and Half, A Number* and *7 Blowjobs* (B Sharp); *10,000 Beers, Drowned World* and *Vicious Streaks* (co-directed with George Ogilvie) (Darlinghurst Theatre); *The Share* and *The Hour Before My Brother Dies* (TRS at the Old Fitzroy); *A Winter's Tale, After Dinner, Shopping and F**king* and *Big Love* (NIDA); *As You Like It* (WAAPA); *Julius Caesar and Trojan Women: A Love Story* (Theatre Nepean); *On That Day* (Short and Sweet); and *The Tempest* and *Our Town* (the New Theatre). With 16 young actors, Lee co-devised *Battlegrounds* at ATYP. She has also taught at NIDA, Sydney University and New York University, and for three years was the director of the NSW State Schools' Senior Drama Ensemble. She has worked as an assistant director on the STC productions of *Riflemind, The Art of War* and *Boy Gets Girl*, and on the Conservatorium of Music production of *Cosi Fan Tutte* directed by Patrick Nolan. She holds a Masters in Directing from NIDA. In 2007 Lee was the Richard Wherrett Fellow at the Sydney Theatre Company and Currency House published her essay *Cross Racial Casting: Changing the Face of Australian Theatre* as part of their Platform Paper series. **Training:** Prior to returning to Australia, Lee completed her MFA in Acting at Columbia University and worked for 10 years in New York on Broadway and Off- Broadway with directors as diverse as Julie Taymor, Andrei Serban, Anne Bogart, Andre Gregory and Robert Woodruff. Lee is currently the Associate Director of Griffin Theatre Company.

Shari Sebbens
Performer
For **Griffin Theatre Company:** Debut. Shari is a proud Bardi, Jabirr-Jabirr woman born and raised in Darwin. **Theatre:** *Wulamanyuwi and the Seven Pamanui* (Darwin Festival); *A Midsummer Night's Dream* (Darwin Theatre Company); *Woman of the Sun* (workshop—Belvoir); *Mash Up* (Penrith Performing and Visual Arts); *Rabbit Hole, Before the Rain, The Importance of Being Earnest, The Kitchen, Measure for Measure, Uncle Vanya, Face to Face* (NIDA). **Film:** Later this year, Shari makes her feature film debut in *The Sapphires* alongside Deborah Mailman, Jessica Mauboy and Miranda Tapsell. **Training:** At 19, Shari was one of 10 young artists

chosen for "SPARK", the Australia Council for the Arts' first theatre mentorship program. Shari went on to study Aboriginal Theatre at the Western Australian Academy of Performing Arts and graduated from NIDA's acting course in 2009. Shari is a proud and passionate advocate for Indigenous theatre, especially the development of new and contemporary works. Through her training and opportunities at NIDA and exposure to Sydney's art scene, she has further developed her love for Shakespeare, film and television whilst maintaining her connection to home.

Glenn Hazeldine
Performer

Theatre: Sydney Theatre Company: *Victory* (dir. Judy Davis), *Tot Mom* (dir. Steven Soderbergh), *Elling* (dir. Pamela Rabe) and John Doyle's *The Pig Iron People* (dir. Craig Ilott). Ensemble Theatre Company: *Tuesdays With Morrie* (dir. Mark Kilmurry), *A View From The Bridge* (dir. Sandra Bates) and *All My Sons* (dir. Adam Cook). Company B Belvoir: *The Judas Kiss* (dir. Neil Armfield). Seymour Centre: *Transparency* (dir. Tim Jones). Bell Shakespeare Company: *As You Like It* (dir. John Bell). His long and fruitful association with David Williamson includes roles in world première productions of *Dead White Males*, *Birthrights*, *A Conversation* and *Rhinestone Rex* and *Miss Monica* and revivals of *Sanctuary* and *Don's Party*. **Television:** his guest appearances include *Tricky Business*, *At Home With Julia*, *All Saints*, *BlackJack*, *Corridors of Power*, *Stingers*, *Water Rats* and *Backberner*. **Film:** Glenn made his feature film debut in the critically acclaimed *Last Train To Freo* (dir. Jeremy Sims). Other film credits include *Dripping In Chocolate* (dir. Mark Joffe), *The Last Time I Saw Michael Gregg* (an experimental project directed by Steven Soderbergh) and the acclaimed short films *Mind's Own Melody* and *The Mechanicals*. **Directing:** He directed David Williamson's *One Night In Emerald City* (Corrilee Foundation), *Stories From The 428* (Sidetrack Theatre) and was assistant director to Sandra Bates on Williamson's *Charitable Intent* (Ensemble Theatre) and to Wayne Harrison on *Defending the Caveman* (Ross Mollison Productions). **Other:** Glenn is a proud member of the Equity branch of the MEAA and sits on the board of the Actors Benevolent Fund of NSW. **Training:** Glenn graduated from NIDA in 1994.

Sally McKenzie
Performer

Sally works as an actor, playwright, director and filmmaker. **Theatre:** As a stage performer, she has appeared in productions for La Boite, MTC, Nimrod, Playbox, Phillip Street, QPAC, Q Theatre, QTC, STCSA, Stables, STC, TN!, and Toadshow. Productions include: *A Conversation*, *After The Ball*, *Alex*, *Amadeus*, *Amigos*, *A Toast To Melba*, *Beach Blanket Tempest*, *Burn This*, *The Changeling*, *The Cherry Orchard*, *Cuckoo in the Nest*, *Dancing at Lughnasa*, *Dinkum Assorted*, *Diving for Pearls*, *episodes*, *Fields of Heaven*, *Fuente Ovejuna*, *Glory*, *The Good Person of Setzuan*, *Hamlet*, *Happy End*, *The Hills Family Show*, *The Importance of Being Earnest*, *Les Liaisons Dangereuse*, *The London Cuckolds*, *MacBeth*, *The Man From Muckinupin*, *Mourning Becomes Electra*, *Money and Friends*, *Mrs Klein*, *Night and Day*, *Red Cap*, *The Ring*, *Romeo and Juliet*, *Salt*, *The School of Arts*, *The Sentimental Bloke*, *Servant of Two Masters*, *Sherwoodstock*, *The Threepenny Opera*, *They Shoot Horses Don't They?*, *Top Dogs*, *Top Girls*, *Top Silk*, *Unsuitable for Adults*, *Visions*, *Vocations* and *The Wishing Well*. **Televison:** TV audiences have seen her as regular Mystic Marg in series *Mortified* and in *The Wayne Manifesto*, *Fat Cow Motel*, *Prisoner*, *A Country Practice*, *Carson's Law*, *The Schippan Mystery* and Cop Shop, for which she won a National Television Society of Australia Penguin Award for Best Single Performance by an Actress. **Playwrighting:** plays include *Scattered Lives* and *i dot luv dot u* ☺. **Other:** Her arts documentary *actingclassof1977. com* debuted on the ABC in 2008 and social documentary *A Woman's Journey Into Sex* will be completed this year and distributed locally by Icon and internationally by Off The Fence. Sally established theCoalface (AKA Coalface Communications) in 1998 to provide programs and services to the entertainment industry. **Training:** Sally has a Bachelor of Dramatic Art in Acting from NIDA and a Master of Fine Arts in Film from QUT.

Charles Allen
Performer

For **Griffin Theatre Company:** Debut. At an early age, Charles fell in love with film and television and wanted to grow up and 'be on TV'. However, with much coaxing from his mother, he chose to pursue a more 'practical' career. While attending university to study the sciences, he stumbled upon an acting class and took it as an elective. His desire to perform was rekindled and thus, the course of his and his mother's life was changed forever. After shifting his focus to the performing arts, he left university, relocated to Dallas, Texas, and pursued independent actor training. While there he performed in theatre, regional commercials, and did background work in films. It was in Dallas that he also made his debut as a stand-up comedian and writer. To further his training, Charles moved to Los Angeles. There he trained under Tony Greco, Beah Richards, and most importantly, Eric Morris. It was with Morris that he found and fell in love with the craft of acting. In Los Angeles he worked in radio, video games, television, film and theatre including performances of *The Mighty Gents*, *Fences*, *A Soldier's Play*, *The Colored Museum*, and *Love's Uprising*. After becoming certified as a teacher of the Eric Morris System, he joined the QUT staff as a lecturer in acting. He served in this role for 3½ years. He makes his Australian stage debut in *A Hoax* and is appreciative for the experience.

Tahli Corin
Dramaturg

Since 2002 Tahli has been working actively as an actor, playwright and producer. **Playwrighting:** Tahli co-wrote *CONCLUSIONS: On Ice* with Joshua Tyler for the 2008 Adelaide Fringe Festival. Her debut play *Bumming With Jane* premièred as part of the 2008 B Sharp season. For Sydney Theatre Company: Tahli wrote *The Arcade* which was presented as part of *Money Shots*, and *Girl In Tan Boots* which was developed through the company's Rough Draft program and will be presented as part of the Women's International Playwright's Conference in Stockholm later this year. **Awards:** In 2009 Tahli was the winner of the Philip Parsons Young Playwright's Award. Her second play, *One for the Ugly Girls* won the audience vote at PlayWriting Australia's Kicking Down the Doors initiative, was shortlisted for the 2010 Rodney Seaborn Award and enjoyed a very successful studio season as part of NovemberISM in 2011. Tahli is currently an Associate Playwright at Playwriting Australia, and the Resident Dramaturg at Griffin Theatre Company. **Training:** Tahli graduated as an actor from the Centre for the Performing Arts (ACArts) in 2002.

Renée Mulder
Designer

For **Griffin Theatre Company:** *A Hoax* is Renée's second design for Griffin Theatre Company following *The Boys*. **Other Theatre:** Also Renée's fifth design for La Boite, following *As You Like It, Ruben Guthrie, Edward Gant's Amazing Feats of Loneliness* (La Boite/Sydney Theatre Company) and *I Love You, Bro*. Additional theatre credits as Designer include, *Sacre Bleu!, Fat Pig* (QTC), *Rough Draft 9* (STC), *The Pigeons* (Griffin Independent), *The Sneeze* (Theatre Forward), *The Herbal Bed* (The New Theatre), *The Hypochondriac, La Dispute* (Sydney Young Actors Studio). Renée has also worked as Design Assistant on a number of productions, including *The Mysteries* (STC), *Good Evening* (Token Events); and within the Costume Art Department on *Pericles* (Bell Shakespeare). **Film:** Her film credits include *A Falling Parachute in Siberia* (Co-Production Designer), *The Distance Between* (Art Direction Assistant), and *Narnia: Voyage of the Dawn Treader* (Armour Art Department). **Training:** Renée holds a Bachelor of Design (Interior) from the Queensland College of Art, and a Bachelor of Dramatic Art (Design) from NIDA.

Jason Glenwright
Lighting Designer

Jason has practiced as a freelance lighting designer on more than 110 diverse and highly acclaimed projects. **Theatre:** *Ruben Guthrie, Julius Caesar* (La Boite); *Faustus* (Bell Shakespeare Company/Queensland Theatre Company), *The Removalists, Water Falling Down, The Little Dog Laughed, Thom Pain (Based on Nothing)* (QTC); *While Others Sleep* (Expressions Dance Company); *Animal Farm* (shake & stir); *Drag Queensland* (Queensland Music Festival); *The Tempest* (Zen Zen Zo); *The Kursk* (Critical Stages/Matrix Theatre); *My Name Is Rachel Corrie, Blackbird* (La Boite Indie), *Tender, The Truth About Kookaburras, The Pillowman, Bronte, The Kursk* (Metro Arts); *At Sea Staring Up, The Shining Path, Cake* (JUTE); *The Neverending Story, The Wizard of Oz, James and the Giant Peach, Jesus Christ Superstar, Songs for a New World, Cinderella, Joseph and the Amazing Technicolor Dreamcoat, Peter Pan* (Harvest Rain/QPAC); *Gaijin* (Gardens Theatre); *[title of show]* (Oscar Theatre Company); *Chasing the Lollyman* (Debase); plus many more productions with independent theatre producers.

Other: Jason has also advised lighting on community lighting projects for Brisbane City Council, including The Stones Corner Street Festival plus co-designed a sculpture included in Sydney's Vivid Light Festival 2011. **Awards:** Four of Jason's lighting designs have been nominated for Matilda Awards including; Harvest Rain's productions of *A Midsummer Night's Dream* in 2008, *Peter Pan* in 2009 and *Songs for a New World* in 2010, and QMF's production of *Drag Queensland* in 2011. Jason was also nominated for Best Emerging Artist at the Matilda Awards in 2009. Jason has also received four Del Arte Chart awards for best lighting design over the last three years.

Steve Toulmin
Music, Sound & A/V Designer
Theatre: Steve's previous work with La Boite includes *Edward Gant's Amazing Feats of Loneliness* (co-production with Sydney Theatre Company), *Julius Caesar*, *Hamlet* and *Attack of the Attacking Attackers!*. Sound Designer: *Scorched*, *The Seed* (Company B); *That Face* (Queensland Theatre Company); *Twelfth Night* (Bell Shakespeare Company—co-designed with Paul Charlier); *Dealing With Clair*, *Hammerhead [is Dead]*, *Arabian Nights* (Griffin Independent); *Bliss*, *Beyond The Neck* (B Sharp); *Me Pregnant*, *Anna Robi and the House of Dogs*, *Rommy*, *No Man's Island*, *Reasonable Doubt*, *The Age of Consent* (Tamarama Rock Surfers); *Hedwig and the Angry Inch* (Showtune Productions); *Four Deaths in the Life of Ronaldo Abok*, *Shakepeare's R&J* (Riverside Theatre); *Beyond The Neck* (Tasmania Performs). Assistant Sound Designer: *Tot Mom* and *A Streetcar Named Desire* (Sydney Theatre Company). Composer: *Me Pregnant*, *After All This*, *Uta Uber Kool Ja*, *Julius Caesar*, *Twelfth Night* (co-composed with Paul Charlier), *Hamlet*, *Bliss*, *That Face*, *The Seed*, *Hammerhead [is Dead]*, *Beyond The Neck*, *Attack of the Attacking Attackers!*, *The Greater Plague*, *Vincent River*, *Arabian Night*. A/V Designer: *Angela's Kitchen* (Griffin Theatre Company); *God of Carnage*, *Tot Mom* (Sydney Theatre Company); *YouthVsPhysics* (the Restaged Histories project). Performer: *After All This* (Elbow Room), *Julius Caesar*, *Our Town*, *Hamlet*, *Cockatoo Prison* (The Tiger Lillies for the Seventeenth Biennale of Sydney), *Beyond the Neck*, *Tooth of Crime* (Arts Radar/Under the Wharf). **Film:** Assistant to Paul Charlier: *Last Ride*. **Training:** Steve graduated from NIDA (Technical Production) in 2006.

Griffin Theatre Company

Griffin Theatre Company is Australia's leading new writing theatre and the home of the best Australian stories.

Formed in 1978, Griffin took up residence at the SBW Stables Theatre in 1980. For over 30 years since, the company has been the boutique powerhouse of Australian theatre: consistently breaking new ground and making an outstanding contribution to the national culture.

Griffin has always been the place to make a great start. Australia's most loved and performed play – Michael Gow's *Away* – premiered at Griffin. The hit films *Lantana* and *The Boys* also began life as plays first produced by the company, as did the TV series *Heartbreak High*. Many artists who now contribute significantly to the Australian theatre, film and television industries began professional careers at Griffin, including Cate Blanchett, Jacqueline McKenzie and David Wenham.

In recent years, this success has continued with smash hits like *The Boys*, *Angela's Kitchen* and *Speaking In Tongues*, and return seasons and national and international tours of plays including *Savage River*, *The Story of the Miracles at Cookie's Table*, *Mr Bailey's Minder* and *Holding the Man*.

Now, Griffin is the only professional theatre company in Sydney entirely dedicated to the development and production of new Australian plays. Presenting four or five productions each year, Griffin regularly tours across Australia. The company also acts as a hub for artists and audiences alike; co-presenting the best independent theatre in Sydney through Griffin Independent; providing audiences with diverse and innovative experiences through GRIFFringe and Griffin *Between the Lines;* nurturing the theatre-makers of tomorrow through our education program, the Griffin Ambassadors; and harnessing the talents of the country's best emerging writers and directors through our groundbreaking resident artist scheme, the Griffin Studio.

Griffin aims to develop and stage the best new Australian stories, in the most exciting theatre in the country, for the widest possible audience.

Griffin Theatre Company

13 Craigend St, Kings Cross NSW 2011
Phone: 02 9332 1052
Fax: 02 9331 1524
Email: info@griffintheatre.com.au
Web: griffintheatre.com.au

SBW Stables Theatre

10 Nimrod St
Kings Cross NSW 2011
Online bookings at griffintheatre.com.au
or call 02 9361 3817

ABOUT
GRIFFIN

La Boite Theatre Company

La Boite is one of Australia's leading theatre companies. Our mission is to produce and present exhilarating theatre that is alive to the present, extends and inspires artists, and invigorates the hearts and minds of audiences.

We believe in theatre, not just plays. We enjoy work that embraces the full grammar of performance – spoken word, movement, music, and the visual arts. We believe in an open and direct conversation between actor and audience: our in-the-round space demands it. This is the language of the contemporary imagination.

We believe in reaching out beyond our walls – to independent artists and teams, to key companies from Australia and beyond, to festivals, and into communities that are eager to participate in what we do. This is what it means to be connected to the world.

We look to new Australian work, fresh international theatre, great texts of the past, and to collaborations with diverse artists and organisations from across the nation and beyond. We look to converse with the times – to unwrap the past and scrutinise the present as a means of expressing our aspirations for the future.

La Boite Theatre Company

PO Box 212, Kelvin Grove QLD 4059
Phone: 07 3007 8600
Fax: 07 3007 8699
Email: info@laboite.com.au
Web: laboite.com.au

Roundhouse Theatre

Level 5, The Works
6-8 Musk Ave
Kelvin Grove

ABOUT LA BOITE THEATRE COMPANY

MAJOR PARTNER

PRODUCTION PARTNER
BRISBANE SEASON

La Boite receives assistance from the Queensland Government through Arts Queensland

In 2010, we teamed up with our pals at Tonkin Zulaikha Greer to give the SBW Stables Theatre a well-earned renovation.

So far we've seen the Stables foyer get a much needed facelift and 2011 saw work start on the auditorium, including a re-fit to the theatre itself, making the seating much more comfy to enjoy shows from and improving backstage spaces, making the lives of our hardworking stage managers and actors that bit easier.

Tonkin Zulaikha Greer are not only a perfect fit for the job with their experience working on a multitude of historically and culturally significant sites, but have also been integral for their vision and their generosity as sponsors of the project.

But TZG aren't the only ones who've been generous; we've had a groundswell of support for the project from theatre fans all around the country and we're so grateful!

But there is yet even still more work to do – Stage 3 of our capital works project will look at some significant changes that will open the foyer up with a new north-facing entrance, improving access and airflow, and accommodating a new bar and cafe.

We will also make a significant investment in an ongoing program, How Green Are We, to make our theatre more sustainable.

If you'd like to help finish the job, email our Development Manager at philanthrophy@griffintheatre.com.au. Donors at brick level and above will be acknowledged in perpetuity in the foyer.

Beam ($120,000+)
Seaborn, Broughton & Walford Foundation

Pillar ($45,000)
Bluptons
Ros Horin & Joe Skrzynski
Rockend Technology Pty Ltd
ArtsNSW
Rebel Penfold-Russell
Kim Williams

CAPITAL WORKS PROGRAM

Step ($15,000)
Antoinette Albert
Nathan Bennett & Nick Marchand
Charmaine & Michael Bradley
Lewin Family
Ezekiel Solomon
Stuart Thomas
Townsend Family

Brick ($3,000)
Anonymous (1)
Gina Bowman, Sally Noonan & Mark Sutcliffe
Baker & McKenzie
BOSE
Gillian Appleton
John Bell & Anna Volska
Jo Briscoe & Brenna Hobson
Rob Brookman & Verity Laughton
Actors Centre Australia
Bob & Helena Carr
Ange Cecco & Melanie Bienemann
Rae & Russ Cottle
Glyn Cryer
Thonet Australia
Alison Deans & Kevin Powell
Richard Glover
Peter Graves, Canberra
Maurice Green AM & Christina Green
The Griffins – Allie, Bel, Jas & Jen
Larry & Tina Grumley
Catherine Hastings
Baly Douglass Foundation
Mary & John Holt
Ken & Lilian Horler
Chris Jackman
Currency Press
Peter, Angela & Piper Keel
Brett Boardman & Lee Lewis
Lisa Mann Creative Management
Wendy McCarthy AO
Sophie McCarthy & Tony Green
Bruce Meagher & Greg Waters
Dr David Nguyen
Dianne O'Connell
Peter O'Connell
Debra Oswald
Anthony Paull
Ian Phipps
Peace of Mind Technology
Celina Pront
Joel Pront
Nicki Bloom & Geordie Brookman
Chris Puplick AM
Annabel Ritchie
Chris & Fran Roberts
Ian Robertson
Mike Robinson
Cre8ion
Will Sheehan
Kate & David Sheppard
Diana Simmonds
Smith & Jones
Augusta Supple
Chris Tooher & Rebecca Tinning

Current as at 29 May 2012

GRIFFIN
STAFF

Griffin donors

Income from Griffin activities covers less than 50% of our operating costs – leaving an ever increasing gap for us to fill through government funding, sponsorship and the generosity of our individual supporters. Your support helps us bridge the gap and keep ticket prices affordable and our work at its best. To make a donation and a difference, contact Griffin on 9332 1052 or donate online at griffintheatre.com.au.

Production ($10,000+)
Anonymous (2)
Estate of the late Ruth Barratt
Sophie McCarthy & Antony Green

Studio ($5,000)
Gil Appleton
James Emmett & Peter Wilson
The Goodness Foundation
Limb Family Foundation
Richard & Elizabeth Longes
Leigh O'Neill
Geoff & Wendy Simpson
Sam Strong & Katherine Slattery

Workshop ($1,000–$4,999)
Baly Douglass Foundation
Richard Cottrell
Ros & Paul Espie
Thomas & Ingeborg Girgensohn
Larry & Tina Grumley
John & Mary Holt
Ken & Lillian Horler
Stephen Manning
Jane Martin
Peter & Dianne O'Connell
Anthony Paull
Judy & Sam Weiss
Paul & Jennifer Winch

Reading ($500–$999)
Anonymous (1)
Jes Andersen
Wendy Ashton
Jason Bourne
Alex Byrne
Elizabeth Evatt
Peter Graves
Michael Hobbs
Margaret Johnston
Lynne O'Neill
Vodafone Foundation
Leslie Walford
Louise Walsh & Dave Jordan
Dr Bill Winspear AM

First Draft ($200–$499)
Anonymous (3)
Corinne Campbell
Michael & Colleen Chesterman
Amanda Clark
Victor Cohen & Rosie McColl
Bryony and Timothy Cox
Max Dingle
Eric Dole
Gadens Lawyers
Julien & Monica Ginsberg
Nicky Gluyas
Brenda Gottsche
David & Christine Hartgill
Belinda Hazelton
Janet Heffernan
Beverley Johnson
Henry Johnston
Michala Lander
Caroline Le Plastrier
Christopher McCabe
Duncan McKay
Stephen McNamara
Frances Milat
Neville Mitchell
Phillip & Monica Moore
Mullinars Casting Consultants
Natalie Pelham
Alex-Oonagh Redmond
Annabel Ritchie
Rebecca Rocheford-Davies
Andrew Rosenberg
Diane & David Russell
Michelle Shek
Ros Tarszisz
Nicholas & Elise Yates
William Zappa

We would also like to thank Peter O'Connell and Jon Clark for their expertise, guidance and time.

Current as of 23 May 2012

GRIFFIN
DONORS

Griffin would like to thank the following:

Government Supporters

Patron 2012 Season Sponsor

Interbrand

Production Sponsors Monday Rush Sponsor

Associate Sponsors

Company Sponsors

Foundations and Trusts

GRIFFIN
SPONSORS

Griffin Theatre Company is assisted by the Australian Government through the Australia Council, its arts funding and advisory body; and the NSW Government through Arts NSW.